A GUIDE-BOOK
TO THE
PRADO MUSEUM

BERNARDINO DE PANTORBA

A GUIDE-BOOK
TO THE
PRADO MUSEUM

INCLUDING A COMMENTARY AND
GENERAL HISTORICAL INFORMATION

TRANSLATED INTO ENGLISH BY
CEDRIC SALTER
(B. A. OXON.)

WITH 96 ILLUSTRATIONS

COMPAÑIA BIBLIOGRAFICA ESPAÑOLA, S. A.
MADRID

E. Sánchez Leal, Santísima Trinidad, 7. Madrid

P R E F A C E

The Prado Art Gallery, locally known as the Prado Museum, is undoubtedly the most notable collection of paintings to be found in Spain. With its 1.700 exhibits it is not only the largest collection in terms of quantity, but also the only Spanish picture gallery of international fame. It would not be an exaggeration to say that no cultured visitor to this country willingly fails to visit the Prado, and the Spaniards, in their thousands, reveal their pride in this matchless artistic heritage.

Owing to its great size, and infinitely varied contents, it is essential to employ a guide-book, and we hope that the following pages will neet this need.

The *Guide-Book to the Prado Picture Gallery* has been divided into three separate sections. The first gives information about the Prado of a general character: the second is devoted to a description of the different galleries, together with some comment upon the best-known exhibits, and the third consists of an alphabetic list of the names of the painters whose works are to be seen, and the galleries in which they may be found.

GENERAL INFORMATION
ABOUT THE PRADO

THE PRADO MUSEUM

The Prado Art Gallery is situated in the centre of the city, in the attractive avenue known as the «Paseo del Prado», not far from the famous Plaza de la Cibeles and the Mediodía Railway Station. The luxury Ritz and Palace Hotels, the Jeronimos Church and the Spanish Academy building are all within a few hundred yards. It is also within easy reach of the Spanish Parliament House (Palacio de las Cortes), Bank of Spain, Fine Arts Club and the Offices of the Spanish Tourist Bureau (Dirección General del Turismo) and of the former Royal Park of the Retiro. The Prado itself faces west, and is fronted by grass lawns and cedar trees, giving it the air of an old palace. In the centre there is a statue of Velázquez.

The south side is also bordered by a small garden and another single statue—that of Murillo. A third—this time of Goya-marks the two entrance doors in the northern front, one on the ground floor and the other reached by a stone stairway leading direct to the first floor, where the best-known paintings are to be found.

The building itself is an attractive example of the neo-classic style, approximately 522 feet in length and 110 feet in width. The general effect from outside is a harmonious blend of the typical rose-coloured Madrid brick and grey-white Colmenar stone.

It was built towards the end of the XVIIIth. century, during the reign of King Charles IIIrd, according to plans prepared by the Madrid architect Juan de Villanueva. It was intended for a natural science museum, but remained empty for many years. During the War of Independence against Napoleon the building suffered considerable damage, and it was not until 1816 that King Ferdinand VIIth. decided to repair it for use as a picture gallery, at a cost of seven million «reales».

The Prado was opened as a Royal art gallery on the 19th of November, 1819, and it was not until 1868, when Queen Isabella IInd was driven into exile, that it became the property of the nation.

It is supposed that the initiative for the Prado's foundation came from Queen María Isabel de Braganza, the second wife of King Ferdinand VIIth, who was a patroness of the arts, but the Queen died without seeing her plans completed.

In 1819 the Prado contained only 311 paintings, all by Spanish artists, the following among them at that time still being alive, namely, Goya, Vicente López, José de Madrazo, José Aparicio, Bartolomé Montalvo and Mariano Sánchez.

The first warden of the Prado, Don Luis Eusebi, produced a simple catalogue, which shows that when it was opened the gallery contained 44 canvases by Velázquez, 44 by Murillo, 43 by the still-life painter Luis Meléndez, 29 by Ribera, 15 by Juan de Juanes, 7 by Alonso Cano, 6 by Zurbarán and 4 by Ribalta. There were only two examples of the work of Goya (who was 73 years old at this time) these being the equestrian portraits of King Charles IVth and Queen María Luisa, both of which are still there today. It is strange to note that there was not a single example of the work of El Greco, and only one canvas by an artist belonging to his school. This is partly accounted for by the fact that in those days El Greco did not enjoy the tremendous reputation he possesses today, and was in any case considered an Italian, rather than a Spanish, painter. Strange though it may seem to us it is only 150 years since Greco was described as «insane»!

This original catalogue contained paintings which were already famous, such as *Las Meninas, The Spinners, The Topers, The Surrender of Breda, The Forge of Vulcan, The Holy Family «del Pajarito»,* Murillo's *Madonnas; Saint Bartholomew's Martyrdom,* by Ribera; *The Last Supper,* by Juan de Juanes, and *Saint Casilda,* by Zurbarán.

The entire original collection of 311 paintings was hung in three galleries on the ground floor.

During the year 1821, 195 works by Italian painters were added, including canvases by Titian, Raphael, Tintoretto, Veronese, Guercino, Bassano, Guido Reni, Andrea del Sarto, Mantegna, Bellini, Sebastiano del Piombo, Lucca Giordano and, in 1843, the first examples of Rubens and Van Dyck.

The palaces of the Spanish Royal Family at the beginning of the XIXth. century contained no less than 5.539 paintings, and the Prado received a considerable number of these during the next 70 years. In addition it obtained valuable legacies from the Museo Nacional de la Trinidad in 1870; from Count Emil d'Erlanger in 1881; Don Ramón de Errazu in 1904; the Duchess of Villahermosa in 1905; Don Pablo Bosch in 1915; Don Pedro Fernández-Durán in 1930, and Don Francisco Cambó in 1941. It is a remarkable fact that there has never been a disputed title of ownership regarding any picture on exhibition in the Prado, nor any case of fire or robbery, though some jewels were stolen from the Tesoro del Delfin in 1918. There is a special studio on the ground floor, permanently at the disposal of a group of artist experts for the painstaking restoration of damaged canvases.

There is an official catalogue signed by the Assistant Director of the Prado, Don Francisco Xavier Sánchez Cantón, which contains a brief and accurate list of all the paintings on exhibition. Enlargements, and restorations, of the building have been made under the auspices of the present Director, Don Fernando Alvarez de Sotomayor.

As has already been mentioned the Prado was not originally built as an art gallery, and for this reason the light is not always satisfactory, and electricity has been employed in some of the ground floor rooms. The small gallery devoted to Greco is badly overcrowded, though those where Titian and Velázquez are on exhibition are better arranged. There are a few paintings which have unavoidably become darkened by the action of time, and a few others where cracks are appearing but, in general, all canvases have been wonderfully well preserved.

Where restoration has been necessary this has been done, in recent times, only by acknowledged experts, though this was not the case at the beginning of last century, when Don Pedro de Madrazo wrote «of the dangerous activities of the restorers of the pictures for the new gallery (The Prado) who, in thirteen months, repaired no less than 297 paintings».

Although the fame of the Prado is founded upon its collection of paintings it also contains many fine sculptures, over 300 of them, all of marble or bronze, being distributed throughout the different galleries. On the ground floor are the jewelry exhibits known as the *Tesoro del Delfin*.

The space available for the magnificent collection of drawings is totally inadequate, and only about one sixth of them are on exhibition on the second floor, including no less than 470 from the hand of Goya. Additionally, the Prado contains a remarkable collection of furniture, tapestry, weapons, ceramics and porcelain, embroideries, miniatures, coins and medals—most of them being legacies from private benefactors.

Of the three thousand paintings possessed by the Prado the 2.270 best are on view there, the others being on loan to provincial art galleries and Government offices. This figure is made up as follows; 830 by Spanish painters, 659 by Flemish, 426 by Italian, 156 by French, 137 by Dutch, 49 by German, 9 by English and 3 by Swedish, masters. There are also two other paintings on exhibition, one by a Portuguese and the other by an artist of unknown nationality.

A resumé of the subject matter shows that, in this total, 867 are on religious themes, from the Old and New Testament or scenes from the lives of the Saints; 470 portraits; 419 interiors; 174 mythological or allegorical paintings; 166 landscapes and seascapes, 118 studies of flowers and still life, and 56 on historical subjects.

The majority of the works on show in the Prado are oil paintings, but there are also frescos; a ceiling decorated by Vicente López; some Spanish and Italian primitives; a few paintings in «gouache» by Pedro Berruguete, some wall frescos by Antoniazzo Romano, Antonio Mohedano and Melozzo da Forli, and some water-colours by Mariano Fortuny and Martín Rico.

The latest catalogue of the Prado shows that some 500 painters have examples of their work on view, of which 120 are Spanish, 120 Italian, over 100 Flemish, some 50 Dutch, 40 French, 10 German and 4 English.

In alphabetical order the Prado includes works by the Spanish painters Benito Manuel de Agüero, Francisco and José Antolínez, Juan de Arellano, Antonio Arias, Francisco and Ramón Bayeu, Gaspar Becerra, Bartolomé Bermejo, Pedro Berruguete, Pedro Atanasio Bocanegra, Juan Martín Cabezalero, Francisco Camilo, Alonso Cano, Vicencio Carducho, Antonio Carnicero, Juan Carreño de Miranda, Antonio del Castillo, Eugenio Caxés, Mateo Cerezo, Claudio Coello, Francisco Collantes, Juan Correa, Juan Antonio Escalante, Jerónimo Jacinto Espinosa, Juan de Espinosa, Antonio María Esquivel, Agustín Esteve, Jerónimo Antonio de Ezquerra, Alejo Fernández, Joaquín Manuel Fernández Cruzado, Gregorio Ferro, Mariano Fortuny, Fernando Gallego, Pedro García de Benabarre, Mateo Gilarte, Jacinto Gómez Pastor, Bartolomé González, Zacarías González Velázquez, Francisco Goya, El Greco, Juan Van der Hamen, Francisco de Herrera *el Viejo* and *el Mozo*, Jaume Huguet, Joaquín Inza, Ignacio Iriarte, José Jiménez Donoso, Juan de Juanes, Fray Joaquín Juncosa, Jusepe Leonardo, Vicente López Portaña, Bernardo López Piquer, Pedro Machuca, José, Federico and Raimundo de Madrazo, Mariano Salvador Maella, Fray Juan Bautista Maino, Esteban March, Vicente Juan Masip, Juan Bautista Martínez del Mazo, Luis Eugenio y Miguel Jacinto Meléndez, Antonio Mohedano, Luis de Morales, Sebastián Muñoz, Bartolomé Esteban Murillo, Juan Fernández Navarrete *el Mudo*, Pedro de Orrente, Francisco Pacheco, Acisclo Antonio de Palomino, Juan Pantoja de la Cruz, Juan de Pareja, Luis Paret, Antonio de Pereda, Bartolomé Pérez, Blas del Prado, Felipe Ramírez, Francisco Ribalta, José Ribelles, José de Ribera, Martín Rico, Fernando del Rincón, Francisco and Fray Juan Rizi, Pedro Ruiz González, Francisco Salmerón, Alonso Sánchez Coello, Cornelio Schut *el Mozo*, Juan de Sevilla, Jorge Manuel Theotocopuli, Alonso Miguel de Tobar, Juan de Toledo, Luis Tristán, Juan de Valdés Leal, Diego Velázquez, Pedro Antonio Vidal, Antonio Viladomat, Pedro de Villafranca, Rodrigo de Villandrando, Pedro Núñez de Villavicencio, Miguel Ximénez, Hernando Yáñez de la Almedina and Francisco de Zurbarán.

There are also a number of Spanish painters who are known only as the Masters of Sigüenza, Sisla (Castilian), Arguis (Aragonese), Estimariu (Catalan), Perea (Valencian), Archbishop Dalmau de Mur (Aragonese), Robledo (native of Burgos), of the Eleven Thousand Virgins (native of Segovia) and Master of Saint Nicholas (native of Burgos). There are also works by Jorge Ingles and Nicholas Frances.

The different schools, which together constitute the best examples of Italian art, are also represented in the Prado, the Venetian being predominant. There are also works from the Florentine, Roman, Bolognese, Neapolitan, Lombard and Ferrara schools of painting.

There is a fine, though smaller, collection of Flemish, Dutch, German and French painters, which give an excellent over-all impression of European art as a whole, though the English painters are rather inadequately represented.

There is a good collection of Flemish «primitives» (XIVth. and XVth. centuries) but only a limited number by early Italian and Spanish masters. In general, the large collection of Spanish paintings dates from the XVIth. and XVIIth. centuries, leading up to the very complete representation of the genius of Goya.

The greatest number of canvases exhibited in the Prado by any individual artist are the 115 oil paintings and 470 crayon or charcoal drawings by Goya. Next come Velázquez and Ribera, both with 50, Murillo with 39, Greco with 32, Zurbarán with 20, Juan de Juanes with 12, Carreño with 11, Sánchez Coello with 10, Claudio Coello with 9, Morales with 8, Pantoja with 8, Alonso Cano with 8, Mazo with 8, Pereda with 6, Valdés Leal and Tristán with 4, Ribalta and Maino with 3.

Titian is the best represented of the Italian artists, with 36 authenticated works, though Lucca Giordano has 28, Tintoretto 26, Veronese 15, Corrado Giaquinto 10, Tiepolo 9 and Raphael 8.

Other Italian painters exhibited at the Prado are: Francesco Albani, Alessandro and Cristofano Allori, Jacopo Amiconi, Fra Angelico, Lucia Anguisciola, Antoniazzo Romano, Antonio Badile, Barocci, the three Bassanos (Francesco, Jacopo and Leandro), Pompeo Girolamo Battoni, Giovanni Bellini, Andrea Belvedere, Giovanni Biliverti, Giuseppe Bonito, Pietro Bonzi, Paris Bordone, Orazio Borgiani, Sandro Botticelli, Il Bronzino, Antonio and Vicencio Campi, Il Canaletto, Lucca Cangiaso, Giovanni Battista Caracciolo, Bartolomé Carducci, Girolamo da Carpi, Agostino and Annibale Carracci, Giovanni Castiglione, Il Catena, Giacomo Cavedone, Giovanni Bettino Cignaroli, Cima da Conegliano, Viviano Codazzi, Sebastiano Conca, Il Correggio, Pietro da Cortona, Danielle and Giovanni Battista Crespi, Il Domenichino, Dosso Dossi, Gasparo Dughet, Aniello Falcone, Cesare Fracanzano, Giacomo and Giulio Francia, Francesco Furini, Tadeo Gaddi, Filippo

Gagliardi, Artemisia and Orazio Gentileschi, Gian Francesco Gessi, Il Giorgione, Il Guercino, Antonio Joli, Giovanni di Stéfano Lanfranco, Bernardino Licinio, Lorenzo Lotto, Bernardino Luini, Maineri da Parma, Pietro Malombra, Rutilio di Lorenzo Manetti, Bartolommeo Manfredi, Andrea Mantegna, Carlo Maratti, Melozzo da Forli, Giovanni Battista Moroni, Jacopo Nani, Giuseppe Nogari, Pietro Novelli, Il Padovanino, the two Palmas *(Elder* and *Younger)*, Giovanni Paolo Panini, Il Parmigianino, Michele Parrasio, Perino del Vaga, Gianbattista Piazetta, Marco dal Pino, Sebastiano del Piombo, Giovanni dal Ponte, Il Pontormo, Carlo Portelli, Mattia Preti, Andrea and Camilo Procaccini, Domenico Puligo, Guido Reni, Giulio Romano, Salvatore Rosa, Francesco Rossi, Andrea Sacchi, Domenico Sani, Andrea del Sarto, Il Sassoferrato, Francesco Solimena, Lionello Spada, Massimo Stanzione, Bernardo Strozzi, Giovanni Domenico Tiepolo, Marietta Robusti *(the Tintoretta)*, Domenico Tintoretto, Alessandro Turchi, Andrea Vaccaro, Carlo Veronese, Gaspar van Vitelli, Danielle da Volterra and Battista Zelotti.

Among Flemish painters Rubens is the best represented in the Prado, there being more than 80 examples of his work on exhibition, if you include a certain number done in collaboration with other painters of his school. Then comes Jan Brueghel de Velours, with 40, David Teniers (Son) with 39, Anton van Dyck, with 33 and Frans Snyders, with 22.

Other Flemish painters include: Alexander van Adriaensen, Denis van Alsloot, Jacques d'Arthois, Osias Beet, Ambrosius Benson, Jacob Andries Beschey, Jan Frans and Peeter van Bloemen, Peter Boel, Jean Baptiste Borkens, Andries Bosmans, Adriaan Frans Boudewyms, Peter Bout, Thierry Bouts, Paul Brill, Adriaen Brouwer, Peeter Brueghel *Elder*, Brueghel *Younger*, Jan de Cock, Pieter Coecke, Marcellus Coffermans, Alexander Coosemans, Jan Cossiers, Adam de Coster, Michel Coxcie, Joost van Craesbeeck, Gaspar de Crayer, Petrus Christus, Cornelis van Dalem, Gerard David, Jacob Fopens van Es, Gaspard van Eyck, Jan Eyck, John of Flandes, Frans Francken *(Elder, Younger* and the son of the latter), Jan Fyt, Antoon Gunther Ghering, Jacob Peter Gowi, Jan Sanders van Hemesen, Peeter Huys, Adriaen Isenbrandt, Jacob Jordaens, Jan van Kessel *(Elder* and *Younger)*, Christoph van der Lamen, Pietro de Lignis, Lambert Lombard, Frans Luyck,

Christiaan Luycks, *Jan de Mabuse*, Jan Massys, Quentin Metsys, Hans Memling, Adan van der Meulen, Peeter Meulener, Theobald Michau, Jan van Bike Miel, Anton Mirou, Peeter van Mol, Josse de Momper, Ludwig Neefs, Peter Neefs *(the Elder)*, Nicholas of Neufchatel, Bernard van Orley, Joachim Patinir, Bonaventura Peeters, Clara Peeters, Frans Pourbus *(the Younger)*, Jan Prevost, Erasmus Quellyn, Jan Reyn, Theodor Rombouts, David Ryckaert, Daniel Seghers, Gerard Seghers, Peeter Snayers, Joris van Son, Adriaen van Stalbent, Ignatius van der Stock, Mathaus Stomer, Justus Susterman, Peeters Symons, Abraham and David Teniers, Jan Philips van Thielen, Justus Tiel, Theodore van Tulden, Lukas van Uden, Adriaen van Utrecht, Lukas van Valckenborgh, Cornelis and Paul de Vos, Roger van der Weyden, Jan Wildens, Artus Wolfordt, Catherine Ykens and Frans Ykens.

Of the French painters, Jean Ranc, Nicolas Poussin and Claude de Lorraine, with 14, 12 and 10 works respectively are the most represented at the Prado. Other French painters, whose works are listed, are: Paul Baudry, Charles and Henri Beaubrun, Jean de Boullogne, Sebastien Bourdon, Antoine François Callet, Courtilleau, Jacques Courtois, Antoine Coypel, Philippe de Champaigne, Michel Dorigny, François Hubert Drouais, Domenico Dupra, Joseph Bernat Flaugier, Charles Joseph Flipart, Charles de la Fosse, Pierre Gobert, Jean Baptiste Greuze, Michel-Ange Houasse, Charles François Hutin, Jean Baptiste Jouvenet, Louis Jean François Lagrenée, Nicolas Largillière, Louis Michel van Loo, Joseph Laurent Malaine, Jean Louis Ernest Meissonier, Pierre Mignard, Jean Marc Nattier, Jean Nocret, Jean Baptiste Oudry, Jean Pillement, François Pret, Hyacinthe Rigaud, Hubert Robert, Louis Silvestre, Charles François de la Traverse, Claude Joseph Vernet, Simon Vouet and Jean Antoine Watteau.

Dutch painters include Anthony Moro with 15 works. Then come Philips Wouverman, with 11; and Bosch, with 7. Other Dutch painters represented here are: Adriaen Backer, Jacob Adriaensz Bellevois, Adriaen Bloemaert, Andries and Johannes Both, Leonard Bramer, Quiringh Gerritsz van Brekelencam, Pieter Claeszon, David Colyn, Coosemas, Adriaen Cronenburch, Joost Cornelisz Droochsloot, Hendrick Jacobsz Dubbels, Pieter Fris, Jan Glauber (named Polidoro), Pieter Grebber, Cornelis van Harlem, Willem Klaesz Heda, Jan Davidsz de Heem, Lucas de Heere, Meindert Hobbema,

Gerard van Honthorst, Cornelis Johnson, Jan Kraek, Gabriel Metsu, Michiel Janszoon van Mierevelt, Hendrick van Minderhout, Eglon Hendrick van der Neer, Pieter Nolpe, Jacob Cornelisz van Oostsanen, Adriaen van Ostade, Anthonie Palamedes, Gerard Jan Palthe, Johannes Parcellis, Cornelis van Poelenburg, Paulus Potter, Rembrandt, Marinus Claeszon van Reymerswaele, Jacob Isacksz van Ruysdael, T. Sauts, Jan van Scorel, Godfried Schalcken, Johannes Pietersz Schoeff, Hendrick van Steenwijk *(the Younger)*, Pieter Steenwijck, Hermann van Swanevelt, Joachim Antonisz Uytewael, Hermann van Vollenhoven and Cornelis Claesz van Wiringen.

German painting is represented in the Prado by Anton Raphael Mengs, with 22 works; Albrecht Dürer with 4; and other painters such as Christoph Amberger, Hans Baldung, Lucas Cranach *(Elder)*, Adam Elsheimer, Angelica Kauffmann, Israhel von Meckenen, Philipp Peter Roos and Jan Christian Vollardt.

David Roberts, John Hoppner, Joshua Reynolds and George Romney, are the only English painters whose work may be seen in the Prado.

Additionally there are the Swedish painters Adolf Ulrik Wertmüller and Anders Zorn, the Portuguese Domingo Carvalho and the painter J. P. de Lioutherbbourg, of unknown nationality. There are also over 200 paintings by anonymous artists.

The outstanding painters not represented in the Prado are the Van Eyck Brothers, van der Goes, Lucas de Leyden, Vermeer de Delft, Frans Hals, Leonardo da Vinci, Il Caravaggio, Il Perugino, Holbein, Grünewald, Gainsborough, Fragonard, Le Brun and Nuño Gonsalves, and there are also very few examples of the Italian fresco painters of the XVth. century.

Very great care has been taken to establish the authenticity of every picture exhibited in the Prado and, whenever there is any doubt on the subject, they are listed as anonymous works by pupils of the school of this or that master. No one, for example, would be prepared to guarantee that the pictures named *The Fount of Grace, Portrait of an Old Man* and *La Gioconda* are not the works of the Van Eyck Brothers, of Holbein and Leonardo, respectively, but they are not exhibited as being by these Masters, as all elements of doubt as to their authorship cannot be removed. The *Gioconda* in the possession of the Prado is in no way inferior to the famous one in the Louvre, and the *Portrait of an Old Man* is as good as any of Holbein's work, while the *Fount of Grace* is equally impressive when compared with the authenticated work of the great Flemish painter.

The Prado at present contains 97 numbered galleries or halls, 34 on the ground floor, 44 on the first floor and 19 on the top floor. While there are exceptions to this rule, generally speaking, the ground floor is devoted to Spanish primitives and examples of XVIth. and XVIIth. century Spanish painters. Also on the ground floor are most of the Flemish and Dutch exhibits of the XVth., XVIth. and XVIIth. centuries, and many of Goya's «cartoons» belonging to the early XIXth. century.

On the first floor there are examples of Spanish paintings of the XVth. to the XIXth. centuries, as well as Italian works of the XVth., XVIth. and XVIIth.

The top floor is devoted to XVIIth. and XVIIIth. century Spanish and English canvases, and includes oil paintings by Mengs, drawings by Goya, and a mixed collection of works by Fernández Durán.

In the main central gallery on the first floor are gathered the most outstanding masterpieces of the whole Prado collection: Velázquez, Goya, El Greco, Murillo, Ribera, Titian, Raphael, Tintoretto, Veronese, Rubens, Van Dyck and Jordaens. Here, too, are the best Flemish primitives, including panels by Dürer, and Botticelli, and others by Fra Angelico and Mantegna.

Perhaps the most famous of all Goya's paintings, the *Maja Vestida* and the *Maja Desnuda*, and some of his terrifyingly realistic war paintings, are also on the first floor.

No attempt can be made to estimate the monetary value of the Prado collection. In 1834, at the death of King Ferdinand VIIth, such an attempt was made in order to divide it between his two daughters, Isabella and Luisa Fernanda. However, as the object of the valuers was to ensure that the best pictures remained in the hands of the Monarch, the estimate was intentionally low in order to enable Isabella to buy out her younger sister inexpensively. As a result their figure of 30 ½ million «reales» gives us no clear idea of its true value. In any case, in the 118 years since then, the market value of pictures has increased an hundred-fold, and the sale value of the collection remains incalculable.

TOUR OF THE MUSEUM

F I R S T   F L O O R

ROTUNDA

Upon entering the Prado by the staircase leading direct to the first floor there is a large circular hall, dominated by a bronze group by Leone and Pompeo Leoni, of Charles Vth. At his feet there is a recumbent figure, symbolic of the Emperor's triumphs over his enemies. This is a fine example of Renaissance sculpture, and is dated 1564. It is notable for the fact that the magnificent armour worn by the Emperor can be removed, revealing a naked body worthy of a Greek hero.

On the walls of this circular hall eleven of the twelve pictures, ordered by King Philip IVth to decorate the Salón de Reinos in his Palace of the Buen Retiro, are on exhibition. These depict various Spanish victories of the period, three of them by an Italian painter who adopted Spanish nationality, Vicente Carducho; two by Eugenio Caxes, two more by the Aragonese painter Jusepe Leonardo and one by Zurbarán. The remaining three, which are the best, are *The Surrender of Breda*, by Velázquez; *The Recapture of Bahia*, by Father Maino, and *The Relief of Genoa*, by Pereda. These pictures, which suffer from poor lighting, are chiefly of interest as the forerunners of the historical painting to which various Spanish masters devoted themselves during the XIXth. century.

FLEMISH AND GERMAN PRIMITIVES

To the right of this circular hall there is a small door leading to a series of five galleries numbered XL, XLI, XLII, XLIII and XLIV, devoted to the exhibition of early Flemish and German paintings. There are over seventy examples, against a background of ochre coloured tapestry. In the first gallery there are works by Quentin Metsys, Van der Weyden, Gossaert, Thierry Bouts, Petrus Christus, Isenbrandt and the so-called Masters of Flémalle, of the Divine Blood and Hoogstraten. In the second, Van der Weyden and Memling are represented, together with a number of less notable pieces by Van Orley, Juan de Flandes and Jan de Cock. The third contains further Isenbrandts, Van Orleys, Gossaerts, Pieter Coeckes and Gerard Davids, as well as the Masters of Francfort and the Divine Blood. In the fourth, there are works by Patinir, Brueghel (the Elder) and Bosch. The last gallery contains examples of Albrecht Dürer, Hans Baldung, Lucas Cranach, Van Reymerswaele, Bosch, Isenbrandt, Israhel van Meckenen, Sanders van Hemesen and a possible Holbein. The collection is completed by a number of anonymous works from the Flemish school.

This collection of early XVth. century paintings reveals the mastery achieved in Northern Europe at that period, and lacks only examples of the work of Jan Van Eyck and Van der Goes (1) to be among the most complete in Europe.

The belief that Huberto and Jan Van Eyck were the originators of oil painting on wooden panels is not undisputed, but there is no doubt that their superb technique was responsible for the acceptance of the use of oils in painting throughout Europe. Their contribution to Art is all the more remarkable as, in their short lives, the brothers Van Eyck not only introduced a new technique but themselves achieved a mastery of it that was never subsequently surpassed. This is emphasised not only by the intense vitality of the works themselves, but also by the extraordinary purity of colour and subtlety of tone that have triumphantly survived the passage of over five centuries. Their precision in representing the design and texture of materials is unequalled in its beauty and restraint. The host of imitators that followed during the succeeding centuries never achieved the same astonishing blend of painstaking workmanship and inspired genius.

---

(1) King Philip IInd was the owner of one of the finest of all Van Eyck's paintings, known as *The Arnolfini Marriage* but, during the Peninsular War against Napoleon, it was sent to England, where it is today on exhibition in the National Gallery. *The Epiphany*, by Van der Goes was also the property of the Colegio de Monforte de Lemos until early in the present century but, owing to the indifference of the authorities, it was sold to the Berlin Museum for the sum of 1.268.800 pesetas.

However, before the Flemish School finally lost the inspiration of its founders, there were many worthy disciples of the Van Eyck brothers who carried on their tradition. Among these were Roger van der Weyden, Hans Memling, Thierry Bouts, and Petrus Christus. Early in the XVIth. century they were succeeded by Gerard David, Quentin Metsys, Jan Gossaert, Joachim Patinir, Adriaen Isenbrandt, Barend van Orley, Jan Sanders van Hemesen, Pieter Coecke van Aels, Hyeronimus van Aeken and Marinus Claeszon van Reymerswaele. Brueghel belongs to a later generation. In the following pages we will briefly examine their works.

HALL XL

There are five outstanding paintings in this room. They are *Christ shown to the people*, by Metsys; *Christ with the Virgin Mary and John the Baptist*, by Gossaert; *St. Barbara* and *The Betrothal of the Virgin*, by the Master of Flémalle, and *The Fount of Grace*, ascribed to the school of the Van Eyck brothers.

Christ shown to the people, by Metsys. This picture was in the collection of the Marquess de Remisa until it was left, as a legacy to the Prado, by Don Mariano Lanuza, in 1940. The first impression is that, despite the size of the panel and the fine colouring, the figures suffer from crowding. However, a vivid contrast is achieved between the serene figure of Christ and the cruel and mocking faces of his executioners, and the robes of a bearded Jew make a satisfying splash of warm red in the foreground.

Christ with the Virgin Mary & St. John the Baptist, by Gossaert. This picture was in the Escorial Monastery until 1839, and it was only then that its authorship was finally established. The influence of the Van Eycks is marked, and the treatment of the adolescent Mary and the rustic figure of St. John the Baptist are strongly reminiscent of the famous Van Eyck *Adoration of the Mystic Lamb*.

The Fount of Grace. (Van Eyck School.) This is an allegorical representation of the triumph of Christianity over Judaism, as revealed in a vision of St. Hildegard. The diversity of detail in the background, both human and architectural, shows the same extraordinary mastery of composition which is the unmistakable hallmark of the genuine Flemish primitive. The three main figures, and choirs of singing angels, are grouped round the Lamb in the upper part of the picture. Below is the Fount of Grace, upon the waters of which is floating the Eucharist. To one side are the figures of Christians, and on the other a group of Jews, blindly turning away from the Waters of Life.

This picture was known to be in the Monastery of El Parral in Segovia in 1454, and then belonged to the collection of the Museo de la Trinidad until its removal to the Prado in 1872. During the whole of its stay in the Museo de la Trinidad it was officially ascribed to Jan van Eyck, who was believed to have visited Spain in 1428.

Before leaving this room we advise any visitor to glance at the poliptych known as *The Visitation*. Perhaps the most beautiful of the panels is that representing *The Epiphany*, which was first ascribed to Petrus Christus, but is now attributed to Bouts. This also came to the Prado from the Escorial in 1839.

St. Barbara, by the Master of Flémalle. This is a delicate study of an interior. St. Barbara is represented as a typical Flemish woman, placidly reading her prayer-book, against a domestic background of homely furniture. It was painted in 1438, bought by King Charles IVth, and came to the Prado from the Royal Palace at Aranjuez in 1827.

The Betrothal of the Virgin, by the Master of Flémalle. For some unknown reason art critics have not given this work its due, although it will bear comparison with the best work of the XVth. century Flemish Masters. It was brought from El Escorial in 1839. The figures of St. James the Apostle and St. Clara on the outer leaves of the triptych have suggested to some experts that the painter known as «the Master of Flémalle» may have been Robert Campin, the teacher of van der Weyden, or even that he may have been van der Weyden himself.

HALL XLI

This room is devoted to the works of Van der Weyden and Memling.

The Descent from the Cross, by Van der Weyden was painted in 1435 for the Chapel of Our Lady of Victory in Louvain. A century later it was sold to Queen Mary of Hungary, Governor of the Low Countries, in exchange for a new organ for the Church, its value being represented as 500 florins, though the Queen also undertook to fill the space formerly occupied by the picture with an exact copy by Michel Coxcie.

Van der Weyden's picture was then sent to King Philip IInd, nephew of Queen Mary, but the ship in which it was being transported was wrecked, and the case in which it had been packed was only recovered with great difficulty. Philip IInd presented it to El Escorial, where it remained for over three and a half centuries, when it replaced another copy by Coxcie already in the Prado.

The Descent from the Cross contains ten figures on a golden background, and an observer is immediately struck by the dramatic quality of the composition, which marks Van der Weyden's work with a deeper religious and emotional appeal than that of any of his contemporaries. Surrounded by the placid and innocent representations of the Virgin and Child so typical of the Flemish school, *The Descent* strikes an authentic note of high tragedy. Despite the characteristic rigidity and exact drawing of Christ's body and His Mother's hands, the whole picture is vital with life and feeling, and the two weeping female figures still further emphasise the sense of drama. It is, perhaps, of interest to observe that the painter had to extend the original panel in order to include the Cross and the male figure on the ladder helping to lower the dead Christ.

Beside *The Descent* there is a small panel named *Piety* which is notable for its modern-seeming brilliance of colour, though the theme is still the tragic one of the Virgin laying her tearful face against that of her dead Son. This work of the artist known as Master Roger was bought by the Prado from the Duke of Mandas in 1925. There is a much inferior duplicate in the Berlin Museum.

The great triptych *The Redemption* was the property of the Madrid Convent of Los Angeles, founded by Doña Leonor Mascareñas, one-time nurse to King Philip IInd. From there it passed to the Museo de la Trinidad, and finally to the Prado, though doubts have occasionally been raised as to whether it is an authentic Van der Weyden.

The centre panel of the triptych depicts Christ on the Cross between the Virgin Mary and St. John, with a Gothic church in the background. The left-hand panel shows the Expulsion from Paradise, and that on the right represents the Last Judgment.

The centre panel is unquestionably the best, Van der Weyden's occasional tendency to over-emphasise facial expression being kept within limits and, by studying it, we can understand how his work came to exercise a greater influence on Spanish Art during the late XVth. and early XVIth. century than that of any other of the Flemish primitive school.

Reinach has written that the work of Hans Memling—sometimes called the Raphael of Flemish Art—is the most original and attractive of the Flemish school. His triptych known as *The Epiphany* was the property of the Emperor Charles Vth, and was in the oratory of Ateca Castle until it was brought to the Prado in 1847. According to some experts it was painted in 1470, and there is another original by the same artist in the Brujas Hospital, signed and dated 1479.

The central panel possesses a serene beauty, and the whole triptych reveals the richness of colour and intricate exactness of design and drawing characteristic of the Flemish school, while the facial expressions reveal a profound study in character.

HALL XLII

The outstanding pictures in this room are *The Virgin of Louvain*, by Gossaert; *Virgin and Child*, by Van Orley; *The Mass of St. Gregory*, by Isenbrandt, and *The Rest during the Flight into Egypt*, by Gerard David, this last providing strong evidence that

David was probably the best Flemish painter of the XVth. century, and worthy heir to Memling.

David's panel is undoubtedly the best of the three in the Prado ascribed to him, and the fine brushwork used to depict every detail of the background is beyond praise. Incidentally, another identical original is in the possession of a British Gallery.

Doubts have been raised as to whether or not the *Virgin of Louvain* is the work of Gossaert, as it differs considerably from his usual style, and some experts ascribe it to Van Orley. Painted in 1516 it came to the Prado from El Escorial in 1839.

HALLS XLIII AND XLIV

The outstanding figure, marking the transition of the Flemish School from the XVth. to the XVIth. century, is the landscape painter Patinir, and his work is immediately recognisable for the unusual green tones which he employed to achieve a strangely dreamlike quality. The human figures only serve as an explanation of the title of *The Flight into Egypt*, and it is the unearthly light shining upon the background which arrests and holds our interest.

The Passage of the Styx is another magnificent example of the work of Patinir, ranking with *The Rest on the Flight into Egypt*. These two pictures, together with his signed *St. Jerome*, showing the Saint in the midst of another unmistakable Patinir landscape, also came to the Prado from El Escorial. *The Temptations of St. Anthony* was made in collaboration with Quentin Metsys, who painted the figures.

All visitors are instantly arrested by the extraordinary nightmare quality of Brueghel's *Triumph of Death*. The whole conception is infused with a profound sense of tragedy, and the brilliant use of greys and greens make it one of the most remarkable pictures in the whole collection. It came to the Prado from the Palace of San Ildefonso in 1827, and is believed to have been painted in 1560 when Brueghel was at the height of his creative powers.

Peeter Brueghel died before he was fifty, so that there are not a great number of his works in existence, and there are only some 30 examples to be seen from the short period of ten years that he devoted to painting. Pleasure-loving, and content with the placid life that surrounded him, *The Triumph of Death* reveals an unexpected aspect of his character.

There is reason to suppose that Jerome van Aeken lived in Spain for a number of years when, finding his Dutch name of Hieronymus Bosch too difficult, the Spaniards referred to him as *el Bosco*.

He was one of the favourite artists of King Philip IInd, as a result of which there are several of his best works still in El Escorial, in addition to the seven bequeathed to the Prado. Probably one of the principal reasons why his works appealed so greatly to Philip IInd—himself something of a visionary, who latterly revealed symptoms of religious mania—was the artist's predilection for religious themes and visions fully understandable only to a psycho-analyst.

Although Friedländer expresses the opinion that the triptych *The Adoration of the Magi* is «the best thing painted by El Bosco», others consider *The Garden of Pleasure, The Chaff Cart* and *The Deadly Sins* better examples of the artist's extraordinary technique.

The Chaff Cart is a triptych suggested by one of the Psalms. The centre panel represents the pleasures of the senses, pursued by those forgetful of the warning that their enjoyment «flieth like chaff before the winds». In one corner of the picture there is a representation of Paradise, showing the creation of Eve, the Temptation and the Fall. In the opposite corner Hell is shown and, when closed, the triptych as a whole represents *The Path of Life*. This masterpiece was bought by Queen Isabel IInd in 1848 from Don José de Salamanca for 16.000 «reales».

The Garden of Pleasure is also in the form of a triptych, and came to the Prado from El Escorial only a few years ago. It was bought by King Philip IInd at an auction of the property of an illegitimate son of the great Duke of Alba in 1592.

The main panel shows a strange grouping of human figures together with animals, birds and fish, which are presumably an allegorical representation of sensuality. The left panel shows the

Cristo presentado al pueblo.   *Le Christ présenté au peuple.*
Jesu Christ shown to the people.   *Christus wird vor das Volk geführt.*

VAN DER WEYDEN

El Descendimiento de la Cruz.   La Descente de la Croix.
Die Kreuzabnahme.

HANS MEMLING

La Adoración de los Magos (centro del tríptico).
L'Adoration des Mages (panneau central du triptyque).
The Epiphany.   Die Anbetung der Könige.

PEETER BRUEGHEL

El Triunfo de la Muerte.   Le Triomphe de la Mort.
The Triumph of the Death.   Der Sieg des Todes.

HIERONYMUS BOSCH

El Jardín de las Delicias (fragmento).   The Garden of the Delights (detail).
Le Jardin des Délices (détail).   Der Garten des Genusses (Fragment).

Autorretrato.   *Portrait de l'auteur.*
Self-portrait.   *Selbstbildnis.*

Auto de fe.

El Cardenal.   *Le Cardinal.*
The Cardinal.   *Der Kardinal.*

El tránsito de la Virgen.
The Death of the Virgin.

La Dormition de la Vierge.
Der Tod der heiligen Jungfrau.

FRA ANGELICO

La Anunciación.   L'Annonciation.
The Annunciation.   Die Verkündigung.

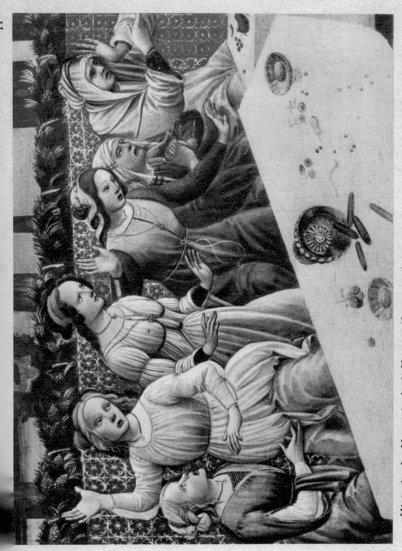

Historia de Nastagio degli Honesti (fragmento).
Histoire de Nastagio degli Honesti (détail).
The Story of Nastagio degli Honesti (detail).
Die Geschichte von Nastagio degli Honesti (Fragment).

Moises salvado del Nilo.
Moses rescued from the Nile.

Moïse sauvé du Nil.
Moses vom Nil gerettet.

Autorretrato (fragmento).
Self-portrait (detail).

Portrait de l'auteur (détail).
Selbstbildnis (Fragment).

TIZIANO

Jesús y el Cirineo. Jesus and Simon of Cyrene.

Jesus and Simon von Kyrene.

Ofrenda a la diosa de los amores.   Offrande à la déesse des amours.
The Offering to the Goddess of Love.   Opfer an die Göttin der Liebe.

TINTORETTO

El Lavatorio (fragmento).   Le Lavement des pieds (détail).
The Lavation   (detail).   Die Fusswaschung (Fragment).

Creation of the World, while Hell is depicted on the opposite panel. When the two leaves are closed it reveals another representation of the Creation, and the flowering of the first trees and plants.

It is difficult to find a suitable title for this triptych, which is usually referred to by the Spaniards as *The Garden of Licence*, or *The Wages of Sin*. The scene is of a wild glade in some tropical Garden of Eden, peopled by naked human figures and strange animals. It is not difficult to see the influence of the recently reported discovery of America upon the artist's imagination, at a time when Christopher Columbus himself was convinced that he had discovered the Garden of Eden at the mouth of the River Orinoco.

In the left panel's picture of Paradise, where the newly-created Eve is revealed to Adam, all the tropical animals, real and imaginary, known to the Middle Ages are represented. Elephant, giraffe and unicorn; flying-fish, giant saurians and birds with three heads. all disport themselves against a background of trees, symbolic of love.

The central panel depicts a thickly wooded glade. Through the branches of this there is a glimpse of a shining lake, along the banks of which there is a procession of human figures, riding astride upon panthers, horses, deer, wolves, lions, camels, bears, griffins, unicorns and boar, followed by the witch-like figure of a Nature-Priestess. The foreground of the panel is occupied by the shapes of vast imaginary tropical plants.

The artist obviously wished to convey the message that the short step between the timeless future of the Elysian fields, and the «unearthly twilight of blackest Hell» is fatally spanned by surrender to the lusts of the flesh.

Jerome van Aeken (El Bosco) painted *The Deadly Sins* as a table-top, and it is exhibited in this form, protected by a sheet of glass, in the same way as the famous *History of King David* by Hans Sebald Beham is displayed in the Louvre. It came into the possession of the Prado only quite recently from Escorial.

Within a luminous circle Christ is depicted above the words «Cave, cave, Dominus videt». Beyond this centre-piece, the panel is divided into seven parts, in each of which one of the Seven Deadly Sins is represented. On the four corners of the table there is an allegorical representation of Death, The Last Judgment, Hell, and Paradise. *The Deadly Sins* was greatly admired by Philip IInd, who ordered that it should be kept in the room in which he later died.

El Bosco used to describe these pictures as dreams, and the German critic Charles Justi remarks «a wild and violent blending of dream and reality, executed in a thoughtful and painstaking style». These occasional flights into a nightmare world of their own is to be observed in many other brilliant artists, such as Callot, David Teniers and Goya. Contemporaries often attacked *El Bosco's* work on the ground that he selected fantastic themes so as to disguise his inability to portray the things his eyes actually saw, but the indications are that many artistic geniuses are haunted by similar grotesque and macabre shapes. Psychologically speaking, these «dream pictures» show his tremendous preoccupation with all the aspects and consequences of sin, and his triptychs nearly always follow the same form; the left-hand panel being concerned with the origin of sin, the right-hand one with its consequences, and the main, central, panel with the unending struggle between Good and Evil for possession of the human soul.

El Bosco has sometimes been called «the remote ancestor of the caricaturist», and there is a certain burlesque quality in his small picture, known as *The Extraction of the Stone of Madness*, which King Philip IInd bought from the heirs of Felipe de Guevara.

Another panel showing the temptations suffered by the patriarch of the Tebaida monks is interesting, but inferior to his triptych one the same theme in Lisbon.

Commenting upon *El Bosco's* unusual personality a Prior of the Escorial monastery wrote during the XVIIIth. century «beneath the guise of pictures apparently designed solely to give pleasure to the beholder he imparts a religious message of tremendous power. The effectiveness of his work lies largely in his capacity for the most exact copies from Nature, especially of birds and fishes, together with a brilliantly conceived sense of fantasy, that often makes it difficult to distinguish one from the other».

Even with only four examples of his work Albrecht Dürer manages to demonstrate his mastery as a portrait painter. There is a self-portrait; that of an unknown man, and two separate nudes representing Adam and Eve. His self-portrait, dated 1498, was bought by King Philip IVth from King Charles Ist of England. Prior to that it had been the property of Nüremberg Town Hall, and also of the British Earl of Arundel, and only reached the Prado in 1827. Perhaps the most interesting characteristic revealed by this self-portrait is the blending of the stern German character with softer Italian influences of light and colour.

The less well-known *Portrait of an Unknown Man* is also in the artist's best vein, and the ruddy complexion, keen eyes, and tightly compressed lips combine to produce a brilliant character sketch. This picture, dated 1524, is recorded in the inventory of the Alcázar de Madrid in 1686, finally reaching the Prado in 1827. At that time the experts were not convinced, as they now are, that it was the work of Dürer himself, classifying it as the work of one of his pupils.

Dürer's figures of Adam and Eve, painted in 1507, first came to Spain as a gift from Queen Christina of Sweden to King Philip IVth, but narrowly escaped being burned as obscene during the reign of the prudish King Charles IIIrd. They were hidden in the Academia de San Fernando until they were brought to the Prado in 1827. Incidentally, various copies of these pictures, containing minor variations, are to be seen in the Uffizi Gallery in Florence. It is interesting to note that these are the earliest known oil paintings of Adam and Eve, with the sole exception of the left panel of Van der Weyden's triptych *The Redemption*.

The *Portrait of an Old Man*, which is exhibited among Dürer's nudes, is believed by some experts to be the work of Hans Holbein (the Younger) and, if they are correct, this Hall XLIV contains specimens of the two greatest German Masters. It is a portrait of extraordinary power, believed to represent Sebastian Munster, but mystery surrounds the identity of both painter and model. There is a copy of this painting in the Philadelphia Museum and, although some critics attribute it to Joos van Cleve, modern opinion is increasingly convinced that it is by Holbein.

In this same Hall there are two pictures by Lucas Cranach *(Elder)* portraying a hunting scene, and two others entitled *The Three Graces* and *The Ages and Death of Man*, by Hans Baldung, but none of these will bear comparison with the surrounding Flemish and German masterpieces. Van Hemesen's *The Surgeon* reveals the characteristic Flemish style, and, finally, there is a rather colourless head and shoulders portrait by a disciple of François Clouet which, being French, seems oddly out of place.

VESTIBULE TO THE CENTRAL GALLERY (HALL XXIV)

We enter this Vestibule by crossing the Rotunda, where four XVth. century Spanish painters profit by a fine direct light. These are Pedro Berruguete, Bartolomé Bermejo, Fernando Gallego and Miguel Ximénez, though there are also two outstanding masterpieces by unknown artists, entitled *The Virgin of the Catholic Monarchs* and *The Archangel Michael.*

Coming direct from the work of the Flemish school, the inevitable comparison is unfavourable to the Spanish masters who, although they sought to model themselves upon such painters as Van der Weyden and *El Bosco,* had not achieved an equal mastery of design and management of colour. Perhaps the more highly strung Spanish temperament is less in sympathy with the extraordinary attention to detail achieved by northern artists.

The Virgin of the Catholic Monarchs clearly reveals Flemish influence. It was almost certainly commissioned by the famous Inquisitor Torquemada for the Convent of St. Thomas in Avila in the year of the discovery of America. From Avila it passed to the Quinta del Duque de Arco, then to the Museo de la Trinidad, finally reaching the Prado in 1872.

The artist of the *Virgin of the Catholic Monarchs* being unknown, he has been given the name of Zafra, after the village of his birth. His second picture in the Prado is, therefore, known as *The St. Michael of Zafra,* being brought to the Prado in 1925 from the Hospital of St. Michael in Zafra.

The war-like figure of the young St. Michael, surrounded by good and evil angels, is immediately arresting, and closer examination reveals a mass of brilliantly portrayed detail. The slimy quality in the skins of the demons, and the metallic shades of the Saint's armour and shield are uncannily realistic.

This picture, originally painted on a panel, was transferred to canvas only after it came into the possession of the Prado. It was painted late in the XVth. century by an Andalusian Master, and again reveals the contemporary Flemish influence.

Berruguete, father of the great sculptor Alonso, was the first Spanish painter to study in Italy, and the Prado contains a number of panels by him illustrating scenes from the lives of St. Domingo de Guzmán, and of the Italian martyr Pedro of Verona. Perhaps the most interesting of these represents the «auto de fe» held in Avila on November 16th. 1491.

XVth. century Spanish painting was still under foreign influences, Berruguete's work revealing the Italian, while that of Bermejo, and Gallego, follows the Flemish Masters, but already it is possible to discern a purely Spanish tendency in search of a faithful copy direct from Nature.

Berruguete's ten panels were, like Zafra's *Virgin of the Catholic Monarchs,* commissioned by the Convent of St. Thomas in Avila. That representing the «auto de fe» was the property of Don Ignacio Jugo until 1867, when it was sold to the Spanish Government and placed first in the Museo de la Trinidad and, finally, in the Prado.

The other nine panels came into the possession of the Museo de la Trinidad when, in 1836, the Government seized the property of certain religious communities. Four of these panels originally formed the altarpiece, dedicated to St. Domingo, in the Convent of St. Thomas at Avila. These are the centrepiece, *St. Domingo de Guzmán, St. Domingo and the Albigenses, St. Domingo's Miraculous Cure of a Young Man* and *The Revelation of the Virgin Mary.* Other panels portray *The Sermon, The Prayer, The Death* and *The Burial* of the Martyr.

Some critics claim to distinguish a certain inequality in Berruguete's style in these panels, and suggest that some obviously inferior sections were the work of his pupil Santacruz, or Santos Cruz. The XIXth. century French critic, Paul Lefort, wrote «the quality of the ten panels is far from homogeneous, revealing one artist clearly more gifted than the other, and it is for their vigorous colour, rather than for their occasionally faulty design, that they bring to mind the early works of the Venetian School».

On the other hand, the German critic August Mayer considers these panels to be Berruguete's supreme masterpiece, and writes, «these pictures effectively refute the charge that Spain produced no great primitive painters».

The best of the series of panels are the «auto de fe»; *St. Domingo and the Albigenses,* and *The Martyr St. Peter at Prayer.* Those in which the inferior work of another artist is most obvious are *The Sermon of St. Peter, The Martyrdom of St. Peter* and *The Revelation of the Virgin Mary.*

The *St. Domingo of Silos,* by Bartolomé Bermejo is of particular interest because of the remarkable beauty of the filigreed background, and the small symbolic figures grouped behind the dominating representation of the Saint. The same meticulous attention to detail is displayed in the painting of the embroidered and jewelled mitre, while the powerful portrayal of the Saint's expression again reveals the Flemish tradition.

This example of Bermejo's work has been described as «the most powerful of any Spanish primitive painting». It came originally from a Daroca convent, being brought to Madrid in the 1870's for the National Arqueological Museum, and reached the Prado in 1922. It formed the centre-piece of the main retable in the Daroca convent, being commissioned in 1474 and terminated in 1477.

The critic Don Elías Tormo writes of *St. Domingo of Silos* «a glance at this panel is sufficient to convince us that Bermejo is not just another painter of religious subjects, but is the first of the Spanish portraitists». It is interesting to note the liberal use made by the artist of gold, which he employs in robes, furniture, woodwork and numerous other details of the background.

Fernando Gallego's *The Blessing of Christ* cannot stand comparison with the work of Bermejo, but it is restful after *St. Domingo of Silos* for its contrasting lack of detail and ornamentation. It originally formed the central panel in a retable of the Church of San Lorenzo in Toro, being painted in about the year 1490. It came to the Prado in 1915 as part of a legacy from Señor Bosch, who had bought it in Paris from a collector by the name of Kleinberger, who had discovered it years before in a church in Zamora. The influence of the Van Eycks is unmistakeable.

In this same Gallery there are a number of interesting panels by unknown artists originally in the Carthusian Monastery at Miraflores, which came into the possession of the Prado at the time of the dispersal of the Museo de la Trinidad. They represent *The Visitation, The Baptism of Christ, The Nativity, The Sermon on the Mount* and the *Arrest and Beheading of St. John the Baptist.* Some critics have ascribed them to Gallego, and it is obvious that they belong to the Flemish-Spanish School and period.

The last picture of interest, before leaving this gallery, is that known as *The Virgin of the Knight of Montesa* so named because of the portrait of the Knight beside the figure of St. Bernard. It was purchased by the Prado for 100.000 pesetas from Lorenzo Albarrán in 1920. It belongs to the Valencian School of Rodrigo de Osona, and was painted in the last years of the XVth. century. The colouring is vivid, and the heads of both the Virgin and St. Benito are finely portrayed.

At this point visitors may either continue on through the Gallery, or may again cross the Rotunda to enter the left wing of the building where, in nine Galleries, numbered II to X, the hundred and fifty best Italian pictures in the Prado may be seen. In our opinion the second alternative is the better, and we therefore continue with the Gallery marked II, devoted to Raphael.

HALL II

In this Hall, against a background of red velvet, a number of Raphael's pictures are exhibited. These are, firstly, *The Cardinal,* painted in 1510 and bought by King Charles IVth, which reached the Prado in 1827 from the Royal Palace at Aranjuez.

It has never been possible definitely to identify the subject of this portrait, the names of Giulio de Medici (later Pope Clement VIIth) of Bernardo Dovizio da Bibiena, Scaramuccia Trivulzio, Alidosi, and the Swiss Cardinal Mateo Schinners, having all been suggested.

Secondly, *The Holy Family (del Cordero)* which is a signed panel dated 1517, coming to the Prado from El Escorial in 1837.

Thirdly, *The Visitation;* a panel believed to have been painted in about 1519, which was transferred to canvas in Paris in 1816. This is also a signed work of Raphael from the Escorial, having been bought by King Philip IVth in 1655. Critics have suggested that one of Raphael's pupils, Perino del Vaga, collaborated with his master in painting this picture.

Fourthly, *Christ's Fall on the Road to Calvary.* This panel, painted and signed in about 1517, was also transferred to canvas in Paris between the years 1816 and 1818. In 1661 King Philip IVth. paid the Convent of St. Maria dello Spasimo in Palermo, an annual pension of four thousand ducats, and the picture was sent by them to Spain at his request, being transferred to the Prado from the Royal Palace in 1821. Again critics detect the intervention of one of Raphael's pupils, in this case Julius Romano or Penni.

Fifthly, *The Virgin (del Pez),* painted in 1513, which was also transferred to canvas. In 1638 it was sent by the Neapolitan Church of Santo Domingo to the Duke of Medina de las Torres, who presented it to King Philip IVth. It reached the Prado from El Escorial in 1837, and also shows signs of Giulio Romano's collaboration.

Sixthly, *The Holy Family*—often called *The Pearl*—which was painted around 1518. This once formed part of King Charles Ist's famous collection of paintings and, after the British King's execution, was bought by King Philip IVth for £2.000. Its popular name arose from King Philip's comment, «This is the pearl of my collection», even though it also reveals signs of the work of one or more of Raphael's pupils.

Lastly, *The Holy Family (del Roble),* which was painted in 1518; a duplicate being in the Pitti Gallery in Florence. It reached the Prado from the Royal Palace in Madrid in 1827.

In the same Hall there are various other pictures of minor importance.

Raffaello Sanzio, or Santi (Raphael) died in 1520 at the age of 37, but before his death he achieved universal success and recognition, being acknowledged as the head of a School of painting which has unquestionably exerted a powerful influence upon world art. Admirers and imitators appeared in many European countries, among them the so-called Valencian School of Juan de Juanes.

Admiration for his work continued undiminished until the beginning of the XIXth. century and, although today less pronounced, he is still recognised as one of the supreme products of the Italian Renaissance. His style can be directly traced to that of his master Pietro Perugino, but he contrived to assimilate all the best qualities of the period, even including that of his greatest rival for Papal favour, Michael Angelo. In later years various of Raphael's pupils and imitators faithfully copied his technique, but none, in our opinion, ever possessed his genius or achieved his mastery of every form of artistic expression, oil-painted panels, frescoes, murals, altarpieces, and even delicate miniatures.

The Holy Family (del Cordero), which is only 29 × 21 cm., is perhaps the supreme example of his work as a miniaturist. Experts may point out that it reveals the influence of Leonardo da Vinci, or that the figure of St. Joseph follows the tradition of Fra Bartolommeo, but the fact remains that it reveals Raphael as one of the greatest artists of all time.

The Holy Family hardly justifies King Philip IVth's claims on its behalf, despite its undoubted beauty and probably, *The Virgin of the Rose* is an even better example of Raphael's style. Critics of all nationalities, however, seem to be in agreement that the *Virgin (del Pez)*, together with his *Madonna of San Sixto*, at present in Dresden, are the most perfect of Raphael's altar-pieces.

The large painting *Christ's Fall on the Road to Calvary* was valued far higher than any other of his works in 1834, when it was priced at no less than 4.000.000 «reales». To present-day eyes it seems too sombre in its colouring, but the authentic touch of the Master is clearly revealed in the portrayal of Christ and the Virgin Mary.

Raphael's *Portrait of a Cardinal* is considered by many people to be his finest portrait, and all agree that it was untouched by any brush but his own. It is the pale and intelligent head of a typical Renaissance Cardinal, a brilliant study of character, revealing a subtle mastery of colour and tone.

HALL III

The most notable exhibits of this Hall are Botticelli's *The Story of Nastagio degli Honesti;* Fra Angelico's *The Annunciation,* and part of a fresco ascribed to Antoniazzo Romano.

The Annunciation, is a panel believed to have been painted between the years 1430 and 1445, and was sold by the Convent of Santo Domingo at Fiesole to the Duke of Lerma in 1611. After a period in the Convent of Descalzas Reales in Madrid it reached the Prado in 1861. It shows five episodes in the life of the Virgin Mary, closely resembling those by the same artist in the Convent of St. Mark in Florence, and also in Cortona.

The two panels by Botticelli, painted in 1483 and 1487, belong to a series of three, of which the other is on exhibition in London, and were inspired by incidents in Bocaccio's *The Decameron.* They reached the Prado in December 1941 as a legacy from Don Francisco Cambó, who bought them from the Spiridon Gallery in Berlin in 1929.

It is interesting to note that this *Annunciation* is the only example of Fra Angelico's work in the Prado. However, it is a worthy one, revealing the inimitable, dreamlike quality which made the friar unique even in the Florence of the early XVth. century. In his treatment of religious subjects Fra Angelico achieved a spirituality—a tender delicacy of expression, gesture and form—which no other artist has ever been able to equal. In the words of the critic Denis, «Fra Angelico used colours that had been blended with the light of Paradise».

While Fra Angelico's work reveals his own deep spiritual serenity, Botticelli's unmistakably expresses the artist's profound restlessness. Sandro Botticelli was a creature of his times, when Lorenzo de Medici's love of splendour was in mortal conflict with the austerity of Savonarola, and his work clearly reflects this ideological struggle. Even when painting religious subjects there is an almost pagan appreciation of the world of the senses: Virgins and

Venuses alike being chosen solely for their physical beauty, rather than for any qualities of spirituality or intelligence.

The Botticelli panels in the Prado were commissioned to decorate the bridal chamber of a daughter of a noble Florentine family, and some critics have expressed the view that, while he was responsible for their design, he left much of the actual painting to his pupils.

The Story of Nastagio degli Honesti is not a good example of Botticelli's work though, even so, it still reveals occasional touches of the Master's hand.

HALL IV

The most notable work here is *The Death of the Virgin Mary*, a small panel by Andrea Mantegna. However, there are also two extremely interesting panels by one of the earliest painters represented in the Prado, the Florentine Tadeo Gaddi who was born in 1300 and died in 1366. They depict scenes from the life of St. Eloy, and were a legacy from Don Francisco Cambó in 1941.

There is also a fresco, by Melozzo da Forli, entitled *The Angel of Music*, belonging to the early XVth century Florentine School. A painting by Giovanni dal Ponte, in the form of a frieze, represents the seven liberal arts of Astronomy, Geometry, Arithmetic, Music, Rhetoric, Logic and Grammar. Each of these allegorical figures is accompanied by a portrait of the man considered by the artist to be most eminent in that particular art or science Ptolemy, Euclid, Pythagoras, Tubalcain (the inventor of the organ), Cicero, Aristotle and Donato or Prisciano.

Mention may also be made of two interesting Venetian pictures *The Virgin and Child between two Saints*, by Giovanni Bellini, and *Christ giving the Keys to St. Peter*, by Vicenzo Catena. The former came to the Prado in 1821, having formed part of the collection of King Philip Vth; the latter—at that time mistakenly attributed to Giorgione—being brought from El Escorial in 1839. There is a duplicate of this on exhibition in Boston.

The Prado is fortunate in possessing one of the world's few authentic Mantegna oil-paintings, *The Death of the Virgin*, believed to have been painted around 1462. It was bought by King

Philip IVth when, under the Protectorate, the collection of King Charles Ist of England was put up for auction. Formerly in the Royal Palace at Madrid, it came to the Prado in 1821.

The grouping of the Apostles around the figure of the dead Virgin Mary, and the powerful portrayal of expression on their faces, the whole scene set against a grey landscape, is extraordinarily moving, and no visitor should fail to see it.

HALL V

This contains seven works by Andrea del Sarto, two by Parmigianino, two by Bernardino Luini, two by Correggio, one by Sebastiano del Piombo and one by Bronzino.

Of special interest is the picture *La Gioconda*, which some people believe was painted by Leonardo da Vinci, though the best critics consider that it is only an unusually fine copy of the original, which is to be seen in the Louvre. The wood upon which it is painted is oak, which suggests a Northern origin, but one of the most generally held opinions today is that it is a copy made by Leonardo's Spanish pupil, Yáñez de la Almedina. It was in the Alcazar of Madrid at the end of the XVIIth. century, and came to the Prado in 1828.

The Florentine painter, Andrea del Sarto, belongs to the period when the great Italian School had passed its best, but his two panels in the Prado are unusually interesting. The first is of four figures—the Virgin, Child, a Saint and an Angel—the second a portrait of his wife, Lucrecia di Baccio, the colouring of which is reminiscent of Raphael.

This portrait reached the Prado from the Royal Palace in 1821, while the other, and far more important example of del Sarto's work, was bought for £230 by King Philip IVth for El Escorial from King Charles Ist of England's collection.

Andrea del Sarto, who was a contemporary of Raphael, also died before reaching middle age and, although this altar-piece is considered one of his finest works, it is lacking in the deep religious sentiment which infused the paintings of the early Florentine Masters of the XVth century, though perhaps superior to many of them in technique.

Parmigianino, who died when only 37 years old, is a severe, accurate, but not particularly inspired portrait painter, and the head and shoulders of a child, by Bronzino, reveals a similar cold mastery of detail, marred by a lack of psychological interest in his subject.

The Holy Family, by Bernardino Luini, displays this artist's usual somewhat cloying style but, in a catalogue of the paintings in El Escorial made in 1574, it was listed as a probable Leonardo da Vinci. Once the property of King Philip II, it was included in the Prado collection in April 1839.

The best known of Correggio's pictures in the Prado is probably his *Noli me Tangere*, which aroused an enthusiasm among the Neoclacissists which today it is a little difficult for us to understand. This particular picture was bought by the Duke of Medina de las Torres from the collection of King Charles Ist of England for presentation to King Philip IVth. It is believed to have been painted in 1525, and reached the Prado in 1839 from El Escorial.

Greater skill is displayed in the portrayal of Jesus than in that of Mary Magdalene, but the «sublimity» of Correggio, so often emphasised by Mengs and discussed by Bernard Berenson, is difficult to detect in this gentle idealisation of reality.

Mention must be made of Fra Sebastiano del Piombo's *Christ bearing the Cross*, which reveals the influence of Michael Angelo. A duplicate of this picture is in the Hermitage Museum in Leningrad, and is believed to have been commissioned by one of the Emperor Charles Vth's Ambassadors. It was looted by Napoleon's Marshal Soult from El Escorial, and entered the possession of the Prado in 1839.

HALL VI

This is the first Hall devoted to the collection of Venetian Masters, and contains examples of the work of Titian, Tintoretto, Palma (the Elder), Giorgione, Lotto, Jacopo Bassano, Moroni and others of the same School.

The Adoration of the Shepherds, by Palma, came from the royal collection, where it was ascribed to a younger painter of the same School, Bonifacio Veronese, and is one of the most interesting of the numerous renderings of this particular theme.

The Giorgione was a gift to King Philip IVth from the Duke of Medina de las Torres, but the colouring lacks brilliance. Similarly, the *St. Jerome,* of Lotto, seems unduly dark. A better example of Lotto's work is provided by the portraits, painted on one canvas, of Micer Marsilio and his wife, signed by the artist and dated 1523. Other interesting paintings in this Hall are the self-portrait of Jacopo da Ponte; two half-length figures, one by Moroni and the other by Licinio and, lastly, *The Lady in the Green Turban,* attributed to Dosso Dossi.

There are further examples of the works of Titian and Tintoretto in Halls IX and X but, for the moment, we are concerned with those now before us. These include the following by Titian.

1) The portrait of a Venetian politician and writer, Daniello Barbaro, painted about the year 1545.

2) *Virgin and Child with two Saints,* obviously inspired by Giorgione's work on the same theme, though the influence of Giovanni Bellini—master of both Giorgione and Titian—is also clearly discernible. This is one of the earliest of Titian's works, and came to the Prado from El Escorial in 1839. The Saints are believed to be St. George and St. Catherine.

3) *Ecce Homo,* which is painted on slate and signed by the artist, is believed to have been commissioned personally by the Emperor Charles Vth, who took it with him on his retirement into the Monastery of Yuste, where he died in 1558.

4) *Christ and Simon of Cyrene,* is also a signed work, believ-

ed to have been painted in 1560, passing from the Alcazar of Madrid, where it was catalogued in 1666, to the Buen Retiro and, finally, to the Prado.

5) *Christ appearing as a Gardener*, painted by order of Queen Mary of Hungary, was cut from the *Noli me Tangere* in 1566 by order of King Philip IInd.

6 and 7) Two *Dolorosas*, one on wood and the other on marble. The latter, a companion work to the *Ecce Homo*, bearing only a part of the Master's signature, is the finer of the two, and was sent to Queen Mary of Hungary in 1554, when she was acting as Regent of Flanders. That painted on wood is believed to have been given by Titian to the Emperor Charles Vth. in 1550, and was in his possession at the time of his death in the Monastery of Yuste. The *Dolorosa* on marble is a brilliant portraval of grief, and was said to have «aroused pious sentiments» in the heart of the Emperor.

The two portraits by Tintoretto—one of Pedro de Medici, the other of a Jesuit priest—are not considered to be among his more important works.

HALL VII

This Hall is devoted to eight pictures by Veronese and, although the lighting leaves much to be desired at certain hours of the day, the unmistakable golden tones of this Master's work are enhanced by the crimson material covering the walls.

These pictures are:

1) *Youth choosing between Virtue and Vice;* one of the artist's early works, of which there is a duplicate in the Frick collection in New York. It is known to have been in the possession of King Charles IInd during the last years of the XVIIth. century, and came to the Prado in 1821.

2) *The Martyrdom of St. Mena*—formerly believed to be St. Gines—was a gift from a Spanish Admiral to King Philip IVth, and reached the Prado, from El Escorial, in 1837.

3) *The Outcast Family of Cain* is catalogued as having been in the Royal Palace in the reign of King Charles IInd. There is a duplicate in Vienna.

4) *Christ discoursing in the Temple.* This is one of the finest canvases of Veronese, and loses nothing from the belief that the background may have been painted by the artist's brother, Benedetto. It came to the Prado from the Royal Palace in 1821. When Ribera was in Italy he made a copy of this picture.

5) *Abraham's Sacrifice of Isaac*, was bought from the collection of King Charles Ist of England, entering the Prado in 1837 from El Escorial. There is a duplicate of this picture in Vienna, which is considered the better of the two.

6) *Venus and Adonis*, believed to have been painted in 1580. This canvas was bought by Velázquez when he was in Venice in 1648 on behalf of King Philip IVth. It came to the Prado in 1821 from the Royal Palace.

7) *The Penitent Magdalene*, dated 1583, belonged to the collection of Elizabeth Farnesio, becoming the property of the Prado in 1828.

8) *Jesus and the Centurion* belongs to the period of the painter's maturity, and came to the Prado in 1839 from El Escorial, having formerly been part of the collection of King Charles Ist of England. Veronese made several duplicates of this picture.

This Hall also contains a *Portrait of a Lady* ascribed to Tintoretto, and a *St. Margaret* by one of Titian's pupils.

Paolo Caliari was given the surname Veronés by the Spaniards after his native city of Verona. He is the third of the great Venetian triunvirate, of which Titian and Tintoretto are the others.

The work of these three artists had an exceptional influence upon Spanish artistic taste and style, directly inspiring both El Greco and Velázquez. They were the undisputed favourites of the Spanish Kings of the XVIth. and XVIIth. centuries, and it was the special enthusiasm for the Venetian triunvirate shewn by the Emperor Charles Vth and his son Philip IInd—especially for Titian—which is the reason why the Prado today possesses such a splendid collection of works from this School.

It is interesting to note that the influence of the Church in Spain confined the work of Spanish artists to religious subjects at a time when the Venetians of the XVIth. century were

JUAN DE JUANES

La última Cena.   Le dernière Cène.   The Holy Supper.   Das letzte Abendmahl.

Un caballero.   *Un chevalier.*
Portrait of a Knight.   *Ritterbildnis.*

San Andrés y San Francisco.
Saint Andrew and Saint Francis.

Saint André et Saint François.
Sankt Andreas und Sankt Franciskus.

La Infanta Isabel Clara Eugenia.   *L'Infante Isabelle Claire Eugénie.*
The Infanta Isabel Clara Eugenia.   *Prinzessin Isabel Clara Eugenia.*

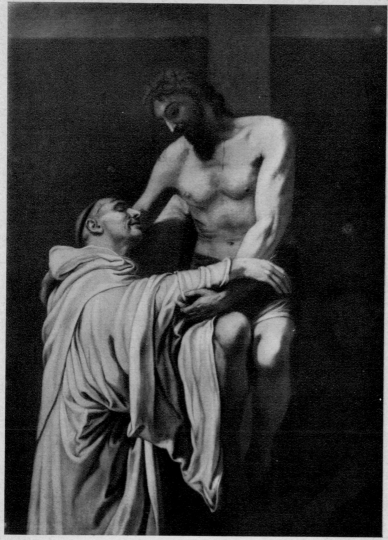

Cristo abrazando a San Bernardo.
Christ embracing Saint Bernard.

Le Christ étreignant Saint Bernard.
Christus umarmt Sankt Bernhard.

Recuperación de Bahía del Brasil.   *La Récupération de Bahia au Brésil.*
The Recovery of Bahia, in Brazil.   *Wiedereroberung von Bahía in Brasilien.*

El martirio de San Bartolomé.   *Le martyre de Saint Barthélémy.*
The Martyrdom of Saint Bartholomew.   *Die Marter von Sankt Bartholomäus.*

Santa Casilda.   *Sainte Casilde.*
Santa Casilda.   *Santa Casilda.*

El bufón D. Juan de Austria.
The buffoon D. Juan de Austria.

Le bouffon D. Juan de Austria.
Der Hofnarr D. Juan de Austria.

"Las Meninas".

Las Hilanderas (fragmento).   *Les Fileuses (détail).*
The Spinners (detail).   *Die Spinnerinnen (Fragment).*

Retrato de Felipe IV (fragmento).
Portrait of Philip IV (detail).

Portrait de Philippe IV (détail).
Bildnis von Philipp des IV (Fragment).

Retrato de Paul de Pont (?) (*fragmento*).
Portrait of Paul de Pont (?) (*detail*).

Portrait de Paul de Pont (?) (*détail*).
Bildnis von Paul de Pont (?) (*Fragment*).

La familia del pintor.
Jordaens' Family on a Garden.

La famille du peintre.
Die Familie des Malers.

Los Niños de la concha.   *Les Enfants à la coquille.*
The Children of the Shell.   *Die Kinder mit der Muschel.*

El Triunfo de San Agustín.
The Triumph of Saint Augustin.

Le Triomphe de Saint Augustin.
Der Triumph des Sankt Augustin.

able to portray the nude in mythological themes. This prudish attitude in Spain gravely limited their scope, and it is only due to the Flemish and Italian painters of the XVIth. and XVIIth. centuries—with their liking for pagan themes—that the walls of the Prado are brightened by the flesh tints of such painters as Rubens.

One feels that religious themes were little more than an excuse for the Venetian School of painters, selected only in order to enable them to display their decorative and pictorial brilliance, and the pleasure that they give to the beholder lies in their rich colouring rather than for any religious sentiment that they convey. This is particularly true of the *Martyrdom of St. Mena,* where the exuberance of the figures depicted obscures completely the tragic theme after which it is named.

The critic, Don Pedro de Madrazo, sums up Veronese's work as follows: «His genius lies in the majesty of the figures he portrays, beautifully grouped in the classical style, and in a beauty appealing to the senses rather than to the mind, through the medium of his masterly use of colour. Veronese was not the equal of Titian in conveying the more delicate flesh-tones, but his luminous colouring, and strange deep shadows, were never equalled by any other of the Venetian Masters».

HALL VIII

This Hall contains paintings by Titian and Veronese. The following are those by Veronese:

1) *The Wedding in Cana.* This is one of the artist's earlier works.

2) *Susanna and the Elders,* which came to the Prado from the Royal Palace in 1821.

3) *Discovery of the Infant Moses on the Banks of the Nile,* also from the Royal Palace.

4) The portraits of Livia Colonna and Lavinia Vecellio (Titian's daughter).

Those by Titian are:

1) *The Church upheld by Spain,* and 2) *Jesus and Simon of Cyrene,* both of which came to the Prado from El Escorial.

3) *Venus listening to music,* and 4) *The Marqués del Vasto haranguing his Troops.* These two pictures, together with Verone-

se's *Wedding in Cana,* were bought from the collection of King
Charles Ist of England.

5)   *Philip IInd after the Battle of Lepanto commending his
son to God.* This was a companion picture to Titian's *Charles Vth
at Mühlberg,* completed in 1575 and reaching the Prado from
the Royal Palace in Madrid.

6 and 7)   Two portraits entitled, *Gentleman with a Watch,* and
The man in an Ermine Collar.

This Hall also contains a canvas by Leandro Bassano, formerly
ascribed to Titian.

The picture *The Church upheld by Spain* is upon the same
lines as the other canvas executed by Titian for the Emperor
Charles Vth, entitled *The Church persecuted by Heresy.* During
the reign of King Philip IInd the theme was repeated by the
artist for the Doria family, which had played a distinguished part
in the victory of Lepanto. In these later versions Titian subs-
tituted the arms of the House of Doria for those of Spain on the
shield carried by the figure fighting on behalf of religion.

The 1949 Prado catalogue relates that when, in 1566, Vasari
visited Titian, he saw an uncompleted portrait of Alfonso Ist of
Ferrara against a similar mythological background. In 1575, after
the Battle of Lepanto, the picture was sent by Titian to Philip IInd
and showed Spain as the Goddess Minerva—a rather surprising
addition being that of a turban to the figure of Neptune.

There are two almost identical versions in the Prado of Titian's picture, *Venus listening to music,* in one of which the Goddess
of Love is embraced by Cupid while, in the other, she is shown
fondling a small dog.

Both have had an interesting history, and were in danger of
being burned as indecent because of the nude figures, while that
showing Cupid was carried off to France by Napoleon's brother,
Joseph. However, both were in the Academy of San Fernando
again by 1818, and came to the Prado nine years later. In 1834
they were valued at 400.000 «reales» each. The canvas containing
the figure of Cupid is signed by Titian while the other is not.

It is not known who commissioned Titian to paint these two
versions of *Venus listening to Music,* but one critic suggests that
it may have been for Francesco Assonica. Madrazo, who believes
them to have been painted between 1530 and 1540, says, «These

canvases can clearly be identified with the famous *Reclining Venus* in Florence, commissioned by Francesco Maria della Rovere, Duke of Urbino, the model used in both being the same. This is particularly noticable since she is of a type not usually chosen by the artist, which suggests that she was the mistress of the Duke. There is a similar picture in the Cambridge Gallery, supposed to represent the Princess de Eboli—with King Philip IInd at her side playing a lute—, but it seems unlikely that women of the Royal family would have been ready to pose in the nude.

Titian's second version of *Jesus with Simon of Cyrene* reveals a more profound feeling for religion than is usual with him. The Christ is not the usual tragic, exhausted Man, staggering beneath the burden of the Cross and scourged by His executioners, but a gentle figure, whose features express only a serene pity for His persecutors. The expression on the face of Simon, as he gazes at the stricken figure, is profoundly moving, and this canvas is considered by most people to be the best of Titian's religious works in the possession of the Prado.

Before leaving this Hall we should take care not to miss Veronese's *Discovery of the Infant Moses on the banks of the Nile*, which, with its rich colouring and masterly grouping, is one of the best of the small canvases in the Prado. There is a beautiful painting by Veronese in the Dresden Museum on the same subject, but the one here is equally attractive.

HALL IX

This is devoted entirely to Titian Vecellio. Red velvet hangings cover the dark marble wall, and provide a magnificent background for sixteen of Titian's finest canvases. These are: *A Self-portrait;* two *Portraits of Charles Vth;* a *Portrait of the Empress Isabel of Portugal;* a *Portrait of Philip IInd;* a *Portrait of Federico Gonzaga, first Duke of Mantua; The Bacchanal; Offering to the Goddess of Love;* a large canvas entitled *Glory;* the duplicate of *Venus listening to Music; Danaë; Salome; St. Margaret,* and the groups *Adam and Eve, Venus and Adonis,* and the *Burial of Christ.*

The Prado is without rival in its collection of the works of three painters—Velázquez, Goya and Titian. Reference has already been made to no less than fourteen of Titian's canvases, and here, in Hall IX, we have arrived at the «sancta sanctorum» of his genius.

On the left, as we enter, there is the exquisitely coloured *Portrait of the Empress Isabel*, painted in Augsburg in 1548 —nine years after the death of the Empress—the artist being compelled to use a mediocre portrait by another artist as his model. This portrait was originally the property of Queen Mary of Hungary, sister-in-law of the Empress Isabel, and entered the Prado in 1821.

Next to it is the technically exquisite *Portrait of Federico Gonzaga*, in which not only the head and hands, but also the texture of the coat material and every detail of the small dog, are faultlessly portrayed. It is a signed work, believed to have been painted between 1525 and 1531. Originally the property of the Marqués de Leganés, it passed to the Royal collection where, in 1666, it was priced at 200 ducats, and thence to the Prado in 1821. It was erroneously catalogued by Madrazo some years later as a portrait of Titian's patron, Alfonso d'Este, Duke of Ferrara.

Next come two splendid portraits of the Emperor Charles Vth, the larger, equestrian one, dominating the whole Hall. Beside it is a delicately executed portrait of King Philip IInd in his early youth and, finally, a magnificent self-portrait of the Master—old and bearded—brilliantly portrayed with a striking economy of detail.

The last self-portrait to which we referred in detail was that of Dürer, and it is interesting to note the great developments in this particular branch of painting which have taken place in the 68 years between 1498 and 1566. While the German painter records his likeness by the precision of his drawing, the Venetian contrives to present us with his living image by means of a few swift strokes of his brush. Titian is known to have done three self-portraits, of which this is undoubtedly the finest. It is believed to have been the property of Rubens, who bought it for the sum of 400 florins.

The Bacchanal typifies all that is best of the Venetian School and, with the *Offering to the Goddess of Love*, is unrivalled in its masterly grouping and for the tender grace of the Cupids. The sleeping Ariadne, and the whole brilliant handling of colour and design, seem to epitomise the artist's own vibrant joy of living.

The *Bacchanal* and the *Offering*—the latter being the smaller picture—were both signed by Titian in 1518 and, together with his *Bacchus and Ariadne* (now in the National Gallery in London), were designed to decorate the famous Alabaster Chamber of the Duke of Ferrara, husband of Lucrecia Borgia. The Duke had commissioned a *Bacchanal* by Giovanni Bellini, but the work was incomplete when that artist died and, according to Vasari, it was finished by Titian. This picture—the work of two supreme artists—was for a long time on exhibition in the Villa Aldobrandini, later becoming the property of the painter Camuccini, and finally reaching London.

The *Bacchanal* and the *Offering* in the Prado became the property of the Ludovisi family, and were for many years in the Panfili Palace at Rome. It is believed that Nicolas Ludovisi, Viceroy of Aragon, presented both works to King Philip IVth, and they reached Madrid in August, 1658.

Rubens made a copy of both pictures while he was in Italy, and these also came to Spain, after a sale in which 1.800 florins was paid for each of them. Looted during the French invasion, they passed into the possession of the Stockholm Museum in 1865.

The Offering to the Goddess of Love was originally entitled, *La Ofrenda a la Fecundidad*, and was valued at 600.000 «reales» in 1834, while its companion picture, *La Bacchanal*, was priced at 400.000 «reales». 13 years later it reached the Prado.

Writing of *The Bacchanal*, Madrazo gives the following description: «In the right foreground the beautiful figure of Ariadne is lying asleep beside a rivulet of wine, her fair hair loose around her naked body, holding an empty goblet in one hand. She is lying on her linen tunic, the end of which is draped across her arm. Beside her a youth and two Bacchantes have laid aside their lutes, while two other youths, standing beneath some trees, are taking up their song. Another more distant group of four men and a woman are dancing around a large wine jar, while they garland themselves with vine leaves. On the left a stout male figure raises a large goblet of wine to his lips, while his bearded companion, resembling an athlete from a Greek bas-relief, bears upon his shoulder a classical amphora. In the background, Theseus's ship can be seen standing out from the shore upon which he has forsaken Ariadne. The artist placed his signature on one of the recumbent Bacchantes, the model for which is believed to have been Titian's mistress, Violante. The sheet of music from which the Bacchantes have been singing has written upon it: «Qui boyt et ne reboyt il ne sait que boyre soit.» (He who drinks but once knows not the joy of drinking.)

The same critic describes *The Offering to the Goddess of Love.* He says: «This is an allegorical representation of the joys and sorrows resulting from love. To this mystic garden two supplicant maidens have come to offer the Goddess a mirror and a votive tablet. From the base of the statue flows a stream, symbolic of fecundity, while the fruit in the tiny baskets carried by the Cupids are ornamented with precious stones.»

Don Pedro Beroqui summed up by saying: «The *Offering* possesses a profound sense of poetry, and is perhaps one of the greatest aesthetic gifts bequeathed to us by Titian, who in it followed Leonardo's maxim: «La eccelente pittura dover sempre accrescere il diletto in chi piú la osserva.» (A great picture must always be a source of delight to those who behold it.)

The critic Frizzoni wrote, a few years ago, that the equestrian portrait of the Emperor Charles Vth «may be considered the finest portrait in existence». To us this assertion appears dangerously categoric, though there can be no doubt as to its exceptional quality.

It was painted in Augsburg during the summer of 1548, in commemmoration of the great Protestant defeat on the river Elbe on August 24th, 1547. Writing of the Emperor Charles on this occasion an historian says: «The Emperor was riding an Andalusian horse, covered with red silk cloth. His armour was shining, and he wore the insignia of a general of the House of Burgundy—a red band, striped with gold—and in his right hand he grasped a lance. He had been suffering acutely from gout and, on the day of the battle, was extremely weak—his enemies mockingly naming him *Carlos the Moribund,* and there were many witnesses of his deathly appearance when he ordered the attack». It is an interesting historical fact that the Emperor Charles always trembled uncontrollably when his armour was being put on him but, once in battle, the delicate body became animated with the strength of courage, and his mind completely serene.

The picture was brought to Spain, together with many others, by the Emperor's sister, Mary of Hungary, and was damaged during the great fire which destroyed the Royal Palace in 1734. Even earlier than this the great canvas was harmed when, immediately after finishing it, Titian left it in the open-air to dry, and a gust of wind overturned it, damaging the horse so seriously that the artist himself had to carry out considerable restoration.

It came to the Prado in 1821, and in 1834 was priced for a mere two hundred thousand «reales».

The other portrait of the Emperor Charles Vth in the Prado is believed to have been painted in Bologna in 1533. King Philip IVth presented it to Charles Ist of England, and it was bought back for £150 at the auction which followed the execution of Charles.

Titian's portrait of King Philip IInd, painted in 1551, was sent by the Spanish King to his aunt, Mary Tudor, at the time of their betrothal. History records that Philip was not satisfied with this portrait, though is it difficult to understand his criticism as it presents him as a most attractive and distinguished young man.

Titian finished *Danaë beneath the Golden Shower* in 1552, when he offered it to King Philip IInd. The artist had already painted a similar picture for Duke Ottavio Farnesio, which was the object of both praise and adverse criticism from Michael Angelo.

Not long afterwards Titian informed King Philip IInd that he had finished another mythological picture saying, «This will provide a contrast with the Danaë, and help to balance its effect in the room for which they are both intended».

This second canvas is a back view of the same nude figure that is portrayed in the *Danaë*, and is entitled *Venus and Adonis*. It was damaged on its way to Spain in a way that is still visible in the centre of the picture. These two pictures, together with the two *Reclining Venuses*, were hidden in the Academia de San

Fernando to escape their destruction by fire ordered by King Charles IIIrd on the grounds that they were indecent.

Titian often used his voluptuously beautiful daughter Lavinia as his model, and we may see her as *Salome* bearing the head of John the Baptist upon a silver dish. It is believed that *Salome* was the property of the Marqués de Leganés, passing to the Royal Family in 1665, and reaching the Prado in 1828.

Although we may perhaps feel that *Salome* rather notably fails to portray the horror of the occasion it represents, it yet remains an attractive example of Titian's work.

Titian's *Glory* was painted in 1551, at the orders of the Emperor Charles Vth, and reached Spain three years later. The Master entitled it *La opera della Trinitá,* and the Emperor *The Last Judgment*. It remained for many years in the Monastery of Yuste, where the Emperor Charles died in retirement, before being moved to El Escorial and receiving its present title of *Titian's Glory*.

The composition of the picture seems over-ambitious for any single canvas. It portrays the Trinity, surrounded by Angels and Seraphs, while below are numerous personalities from both the New and Old Testaments, such as Noah, Moses, David, Job, the Evangelists, and Mary Magdalene. On the right hand side of the picture can be seen the shrouded figures of Charles Vth and his Empress, Philip IInd, Queen Mary of Hungary, and the Infanta Juana. The figure of each sinner on trial is accompanied by his guardian angel, who pleads in his defence.

Despite the sombre subject chosen by the Emperor it gives yet another opportunity to the artist to display his brilliant and colourful style.

There are two versions of *The Burial of Christ,* both signed by Titian, the better of the two being that on exhibition here, which was ordered by King Philip IInd in 1559. A third one, which in our opinion is even more moving, is to be seen in the Louvre.

Titian's *St. Margaret,* and his group *Adam and Eve*—the latter signed by him—belong to the last period of the Master's life, when his style conformed to less exact principles.

Other pictures by Titian may be seen on the first floor of the Prado.

HALL X

This Hall is devoted to Jacopo Robusti, universally known under his brush name of Tintoretto, adopted by him in acknowledgment of his father's profession as a dyer. He is regarded as the most dynamic of the Venetian School of painters and, despite his early poverty, lived to enjoy success and wealth.

Early in his career, Tintoretto outlined his ambition as, «the unification of Michael Angelo's drawing with Titian's use of colour». Whether or not he achieved this tremendous objective must remain a matter of opinion, but it is fairly generally agreed that Tintoretto, in the best of his work, proved himself to be one of the very greatest of the many painters produced by Italy.

Every one of Tintoretto's canvases in the Prado bears witness to his creative genius, though perhaps he never quite achieved the matchless golden hues of Titian, nor the almost mathematical exactness of design peculiar to Michael Angelo, but Tintoretto still possessed an amazing spontaneity—a kind of artistic passion—which gives to all his work an unique inspirational vitality.

This extraordinary verve seemed to carry Tintoretto over all technical obstacles, and is particularly evident on the large surfaces possible in wall painting, where his style is seen at its best.

It has been remarked that nearly all great painters fall into one of two groups, those who seek the warm golds and reds of Titian, Rubens and Rembrandt, or those who sought their ideal medium in the cold grey and sepia tones of Velázquez, Greco and Tintoretto.

The Prado contains 12 portraits and 14 other canvases by Tintoretto. Nine of these were bought by Velázquez in Venice in 1649; two—*Disciples Bathing their Feet*, and *Paradise*— immediately arresting the attention of any visitor to his Hall, both for their great size and their powerful drawing.

In our opinion, the better is *Disciples Bathing their Feet* —originally painted for the Venetian Church of St. Marcuola— which is an unusually vigorous picture with great attention devoted to the background. In the XVIIth century, Father Santos wrote of this work: «The extraordinary vigour of the colours and, above all, the artist's brilliant arrangement of perspective, makes it easy to forget that we are looking at a picture, and creates the sensation that we can enter into the world that it portrays, ourselves walking through the paved court in company with the figures that the artist has portrayed.»

This work was bought at the auction of King Charles Ist's collection, for £250. Velázquez personally arranged for its installation at El Escorial, and it was brought to the Prado only a few years ago.

Paradise—sometimes given the title *Glory*—is not one of the many preparatory sketches made by Tintoretto before he painted his large *Il Paradiso* for the Ducal Palace in Venice. It belongs to the last epoch of the Master, and was bought in Venice by Velázquez. It is in the form of a frieze, nearly 18 feet long by some 4'6" in height, crowded with so many figures that it is not easy to separate one group from another. It is dominated by the grey tones typical of Tintoretto, but suffers from being placed near the ceiling, above other pictures by him, which makes it difficult to study in detail.

It was also due to Velázquez that seven works by Tintoretto, designed to decorate the ceiling of a Venetian palace, are today in the Prado. The themes selected by the artist were from the Old Testament, and the date at which they were painted is not known. The titles given to these pictures are as follows: *The Purification of the Booty, Susanna and the Elders, Esther in the presence of Asuero, Judith and Holofernes, Queen Sheba's visit to Solomon, Joseph and Potiphar's Wife* and *The Discovery of the Infant Moses*.

According to the catalogue, this series belongs to the first period of the artist's life, with the exception of the oval canvas —*The Purification*—which formed the centre piece, and which is believed to have been painted around 1570 when Tintoretto was already over 50. After their arrival in Spain these seven canvases decorated the ceiling of a bedroom in the old Alcázar de Madrid.

They were saved from the destruction by fire of the old Royal Palace in 1734, when they were removed to La Granja, coming to the Prado in 1821.

The oil painting *The Purification*, is typical of Tintoretto's sweeping grey tones, and the other six canvases reveal his almost careless-seeming brilliance of technique.

Another of Tintoretto's pictures brought to Spain by Velázquez is the *Battle between Turks and Christians* which, in our opinion, is not one of the better examples of the Master's work. His *Baptism of Christ*, although rather dark, is a rythmical composition in which certain similarities to Greco have been detected. It was originally painted for the Venetian Church of San Silvestre.

The *Woman Baring her Breast* is almost modern in its treatment and colouring, even while the head maintains the characteristics of a portrait. It is not known for certain who was the model, some critics believing that it was the painter's daughter Marietta, though others believe it to have been a famous courtesan, Veronica Franco.

Tintoretto's *Knight of the Golden Chain*, is believed to be a portrait of Paolo Veronese. In our opinion it is not so fine a work as Tintoretto's portrait of Sebastiano Veniero, which is to be found on the first floor of the Prado.

On exhibition in this Hall is a centre piece for the decoration of a ceiling painted by Tintoretto's son Domenico and entitled *Virtue Triumphing over Sin*. The Sins depicted are Lust, Spite, Treachery and Theft, which are shown in flight from the presence of Virtue, which is represented as a helmeted figure, bearing a sheaf of corn as an emblem of Peace.

Having now seen works by Titian, Veronese and Tintoretto, we must appreciate the debt we owe to the good taste in matters of Art displayed by four of the Hapsburg Kings of Spain. It is solely due to the Emperor Charles Vth. and to Kings Philip IInd, IIIrd and IVth that the Prado today possesses one of the finest collections of the Venetian School to be found anywhere in the world. Only by a study of them can we fully understand the background that inspired the work of El Greco and Velázquez.

HALL XXX

This Hall is devoted to El Greco, but is really too small for the 32 examples of his work that it contains, consisting of 22 on religious themes and 10 portraits.

Greco's prestige has waxed and waned in a remarkable way. Highly valued during his own life, his style ran contrary to current opinion in the succeeding centuries, and only in recent times has it reached the pinnacle upon which it stands today. Even now he is still a painter who provokes violent differences of opinion, some people being rapturous about everything painted by him, while others find his style actively repellent.

Unquestionably, after looking at a number of canvases by other artists, with their more or less conventional methods of presenting the human figure, it does come as something of a shock to be placed suddenly before one of Greco's portraits, with its small, oval head above an immensely elongated body, and this feeling is further emphasised by his unusual employment of colour. There are many who claim to see nothing but deformed shapes and caricatured likenesses but, in the case of all but a very few, reflection reveals the profound vision of the artist, which triumphs over—and is, in fact, emphasised by—the unique methods employed by El Greco.

The essential factor to remember is that El Greco never even sought to paint reality, but only to transfer to canvas the state of mind, or character, of his subject. In short, though he lived centuries before the word was invented, Greco was the first of the Impressionists.

Domenikos Theotokopoulos was a Cretan who learned the art of painting in Venice at a time when Titian, though a very old man, was still living, and when Jacopo Robusti (Tintoretto) was in his prime, and the latter's disregard for the accepted conventions of painting unquestionably had a strong influence upon El Greco. However, the popular belief that Greco originally adopted his individualistic style because he was in revolt against the conventional methods of Titian is not justified.

In fact, what happened was that after Greco had learned all that the Venetian School, as represented by Tintoretto, had to teach him, he came to Spain, where he developed its latest trends along strongly personal lines—so personal as at times almost to suggest insanity. The result was an intensely Spanish product, mystical and passionate, which seems to infuse his figures with a strange inner vibration, as though some occult power was withdrawing the soul from the already exhausted bodies.

To understand Greco, it is necessary to leave the world of design and form, and enter that of spiritual ideas. If we can achieve this the dynamic force behind the vivid, yet trembling, line of his figures reveals the unquiet mind or spirit of the subject as no other painter has ever succeeded in doing. Once this is experienced it is difficult to return to the conventional pink and white portraits of the living flesh which, by contrast, seem hopelessly insipid.

Neither of Greco's two greatest pictures are in the Prado, these being *The Burial of the Count of Orgaz,* and *The Martyrdom of St. Maurice,* but there are a sufficient number here to enable us to form a comprehensive idea of his work. Though his very earliest paintings are still mostly in Italy, the Prado contains examples from each one of the different phases through which his painting passed during his life in Spain.

One of Greco's biographers divides the Artist's work into the following periods: first, from the year 1577 until 1584, which was immediately after his arrival in Spain; the second—and probably the greatest—from 1584 to 1604, and the last until his death in 1614.

Of the pictures by El Greco in the possession of the Prado the following belong to the first period:
The Trinity, The Annunciation, Portrait of a Physician and *The Knight with his Hand on his Breast.* Of these *The Trinity* is known to have been painted for the Church of Saint Domingo in Toledo not later than 1579, when his work for the altar retable

there ended, and is probably the earliest of all Greco's works in the Prado.

Five more belong to the second period of 1584-1594, being two *Portraits of an Unknown Man* (Nos. 806 and 813), *St. Benito, The Crucifixion* and *The Resurrection.* There are some critics who believe that these last two canvases belong to a later period.

It seems fairly certain that the following 12 works were completed between 1594 and 1604: *Portrait of Don Rodrigo Vazquez, St. Paul, St. Anthony of Padua, St. John the Evangelist, Christ Bearing the Cross;* the head and shoulders *Virgin Mary, The Divine Countenance, The Baptism of Christ, The Holy Family, The Coronation of the Virgin Mary* and also *A Santiaguista with St. Louis King of France,* and *St. John the Evangelist and St. Francis of Assisi.*

Finally, painted in the last 10 years of Greco's life, there are two *Portraits of an Unknown Gentleman* (Nos. 810 and 811), *Jerónimo de Cevallos, Portrait of a Monk*—believed to be of the painter Maino—*St. Francis of Assisi with Friar Leone,* and *Pentecost.*

The Prado also contains the following canvases by El Greco which it has been impossible to assign to any particular period in the artist's life: *St. Andrew and St. Francis,* and the three head and shoulder paintings entitled *Jesus, St. James the Elder* and *St. Philip and St. Paul.* In order to appreciate the essential quality of Greco's religious paintings it is only necessary to study *The Trinity, The Annunciation, Christ Bearing the Cross;* the figures of *St. Francis and St. Andrew, The Resurrection, The Crucifixion, The Baptism of Christ* and *Pentecost.* In all these the artist's unique manner of emphasising the spiritual, rather than the physical, characteristics of his subjects are to be seen. The elongated figures, whose bodily existence seems to be in process of visible withdrawal from the world of the flesh into that of the spirit, are the portrayal of something which no other artist has ever even attempted, let alone achieved.

Then there are Greco's portraits, of which he painted very few, mostly of men. There are eight in the Prado, all of them painted while the artist lived in Toledo, which reveal the slender and austere countenances of the Castilian aristocracy at the time when Spain was at the peak of her power.

In our opinion, the finest is the *Head of an Unknown Gentleman*, numbered 806, which is a far more masterly presentation of character than the more famous *Knight with his Hand on his Breast*, where the artist's genius was devoted to the portrayal of the hand rather than to the face of his model. Next to the *Portrait of an Unknown Gentleman*, perhaps the three best are those of *Jerónimo de Cevallos*, *The Unknown Physician* and the small canvas of a monk, all of which, while clearly marked by Greco's characteristic style, are intensely «alive». The half-length *Unknown Physician* is particularly effective in its sober austerity of black, white and ochre. Probably the poorest of Greco's portraits in the Prado is that of Don Rodrigo Vázquez, where both colour and design appear unconvincing.

All 8 of Greco's portraits came here from one or other of the Royal collections—two from the Alcázar de Madrid, and the other six from the country house of the Dukes of Arcos, formerly the property of the King. Five of the eight are signed, and one of them is known to have been in the studio of Velázquez at the time of that artist's death in 1660.

The following of Greco's canvases reached the Prado from the Museo de la Trinidad in 1872: *St. Benito, St. Francis and St. John the Evangelist, St. Anthony of Padua, St. Francis of Assisi with Friar Leone, Christ Bearing the Cross, The Baptism of Christ, The Resurrection, Pentecost* and *The Crucifixion.* All but the first two of these are signed by the artist.

The Trinity was bought for 15.000 «reales» by King Ferdinand VIIth. from the sculptor Valeriano Salvatierra in 1827, and is not catalogued in the Prado until 1843.

The Annunciation was bought in 1868 by Doña Concepción Parody for 150 «escudos», and *St. John the Evangelist* was presented to the Prado in 1921 by Doctor Cabañas. *St. Paul* was in the Royal collection and, after the destruction by fire of the Alcázar in 1734, hung in the Retiro Palace, first appearing in the Prado catalogue for the year 1858. *The Santiaguista with St. Louis, King of France*, which has suffered at the hands of restorers, was bequeathed to the Prado by Don Luis de Errazu in 1926, and *The Coronation of the Virgin Mary*, together with the possible portrait of Maino, were also recent legacies.

The *St. Andrew and St. Francis*, although signed by the artist, was completely unknown until 1937. It was presented to the Madrid Monastery of the Encarnación in 1676 by a daughter of the Duke of Abrantes when she became a nun, and it entered the Prado in 1942. *The Holy Countenance* came to the Prado in 1944 from the Mostoles Church, where its presence had been noted by Cossío.

The Saviour, St. James the Elder and *St. Philip and St. Paul* —all unknown until recent times—were acquired as late as 1946.

The canvas *St. Andrew and St. Francis*, showing the standing figures of the two Saints, is the equal of any of Greco's religious paintings. Here there is his special use of brilliant, yet cold, colours, and the strange elongation of the bodies, giving them the intense, yet deathlike, air with which the artist envisaged the heroes of Christian legend. With the possible exception of Fra Angelico there is no other artist in all the Prado collection who reveals Greco's capacity for depicting the purely spiritual feelings of his subjects. Greco rarely used a human model, drawing his saints from his own imagination, half-dream, half-fantasy. On the other hand, a Saint painted by Ribera, Murillo, Zurbarán or Ribalta —not to mention countless non-Spanish artists—is nearly always a faithful copy of the man who served as his model. Not for nothing was Greco known as the «painter of souls». During the XVIIIth. and XIXth. centuries Greco's prestige sunk very low indeed, and there is hardly a critic of the period who does not refer disparagingly to the peculiarities of his style. Ponz, Ceán Bermúdez and the Madrazo brothers, all spoke of him with distaste, and Cruzada Villaamil wrote in the 1865 catalogue of the Museo de la Trinidad: «It is obvious that El Greco was insane, and his works clearly reveal the extent of his madness even though, behind his weird exaggerations, there are indications, in his handling of colour and portrayal of expression, of genius such as has been possessed by only the greatest Masters.»

In the Prado's 1872 catalogue Don Pedro de Madrazo wrote of Greco: «He suddenly changed the style that he had acquired from studying Titian, and began to paint as though he were a madman. Some people believe that the change was provoked by a desire to demonstrate his complete originality but, whatever the motives, he totally changed his style and developed a fantastic manner of drawing which, together with the use of livid colour-

Juego de niños.   Jeux d'enfants.
Children at Play.   Kinderspiele.

RUBENS

El Jardín del Amor.   Le Jardin de l'Amour.
The Garden of Love.   Der Garten der Liebe.

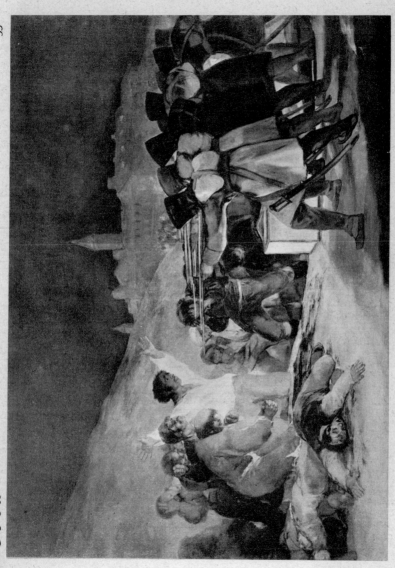

Los fusilamientos de la Moncloa. *Les fusillements de la Moncloa.*
The Firing-Squad in la Moncloa. *Erschiessungen bei der Moncloa.*

Retrato de Francisco Bayeu.
Portrait of Francis Bayeu.

Portrait de François Bayeu.
Bildnís von Franz Bayeu.

La Reina Doña María Cristina de Borbón.
The Queen Maria Cristina de Borbon.

La Reine Marie Christine de Bourbon.
Königin Maria Cristina von Borbon.

Angel portador de la Eucaristía.
Angel bearing the Eucharist.

Ange porteur de l'Eucharistie.
Engel, Träger der Eucharistie.

Retablo de S. Juan Bautista y Sta. Catalina.
Rétable de St. Jean Baptiste et Ste. Catherine.
Retablo of St. John Baptist and St. Catherine.
Altartafel von St. Johannes des Täufers u. Heil. Catharine.

La Reina Maria de Inglaterra.   *La Reine Marie d'Angleterre.*
The Queen Mary of England.   *Königin Maria von England.*

La Virgen y el Niño.   *La Vierge et l'Enfant.*
Virgin with the Child.   *Die Jungfrau und das Kind.*

DAVID TENIERS

Fiesta campestre.   Une fête champêtre.
A Country Party.   Das Fest auf dem Lande.

La familia de Felipe V.   *La famille de Philippe V.*
The Family of Philip V.   *Die Familie Philipps V.*

POUSSIN

El Parnaso.   Le Parnasse.   The Parnassus.   Der Parnassus.

La Sagrada Familia "del Pajarito".   La Sainte Famille "à l' Oiselet".
The Holy Family.   Die Heilige Familie.

La Vendimia.   *La Vendange.*
The Vintage.   *Die Weinernte.*

ing, presented his subjects as though they were half-spectres, half-nightmares, in a way which is particularly noticeable in his *St. Maurice*».

Later, Don Federico de Madrazo, who in 1881 was Director of the Prado, revealed to Justi his disgust at his inability to remove what he called, «the absurd El Greco caricatures».

There have been many attempts to find a purely material explanation for Greco's strange attenuated figures, one of them being that he suffered from some defect in his eye-sight, which caused him to see his fellow-creatures in the distorted form which he portrays.

Such explanations, though attractively simple, are never convincing, and what the neo-classicists called Greco's «madness» is today revered as his «profound psychological perception».

The modern view is that, in order to depict the super-human spiritual qualities of saint and martyr, Greco evolved a mystical technique of his own which, since it dealt with other-worldly subjects, could not be limited by the accepted rules and regulations that suffice for those who seek only to portray the material world of the flesh.

Although the seed of Greco's style may be detected in the Venetian School, he evolved into something unique. Not only is this true of his design and drawing, but also of his use of colour. At a time when all the world was striving to imitate the warm golden hues of the Venetian School, Greco first—and later Velázquez—selected cold blues, greys and sepias to achieve his effects. To appreciate this to the full it is perhaps necessary to see *St. Maurice* and *The Dream of Philip IInd,* which are still in the Monastery of El Escorial—though there is reason to hope that they will soon be added to the Prado collection.

Don Jerónimo Seisdedos, one of the group of skilled restorers employed in the Prado, is of the opinion that Greco treated his canvases with distemper, following the system of the Venetian School, and only used oil for the final touches. Probably for this reason all of Greco's works are today in the same condition as they were nearly three and a half centuries ago.

After the visit to Greco's Hall (No. XXX) it is, in our view, better not to go straight on to a study of Velázquez. We have,

5

therefore, preferred to take a glance at Sections XXV and XXVI in the Prado's great Central Gallery, where are to be found the Spanish artists who immediately preceded Velázquez, namely, Yáñez de la Almedina, Machuca, Juan de Juanes, Sánchez Coello, Ribalta, Pantoja, Maino, Ribera, Van der Hamen, Zurbarán, Felipe Ramírez, Friar Juan Rizi, Juan de Espinosa and Pereda.

CENTRAL GALLERY

SECTIONS XXV AND XXVI

Hernando Yáñez de la Almedina is one of the XVIth. century Spanish painters who most faithfully reflects the lessons of the Italian Renaissance. Although a disciple of Leonardo da Vinci, and with his Master's exquisite presentation of detail, his work has a distinctive quality of its own, which is immediately obvious in his splendid panel *St. Catherine*, once the property of the Marqués de Casa Argudin, and which reached the Prado in 1946. The vivid red of the Saint's robe, and the masterly design of the figure as a whole, mark it as a work of the highest order.

On the Ground Floor there is another vigorous half-length painting by Yáñez entitled *St. Damian*, concerning which we shall have more to say later.

Pedro Machuca was not only a painter, but also a sculptor and architect, and the only example of his work in the possession of the Prado is his *Virgin Mary Comforting the Souls in Purgatory*, which was painted in Italy in 1517, and came to Spain direct from Spoleto in 1935. Don Manuel Gómez Moreno, who made a special study of Machuca, says: «Machuca is clearly not a genius, but he does not lack originality, and devoted great pains in his employment of colour. The tones of the panel are cold, but the work is finely finished.»

Juan de Juanes was known as «the Spanish Rafael», but his picture, *The Last Supper*, possesses little outstanding merit. His reputation, which once stood very high, has fallen in recent times, though a male portrait by him in the same gallery gives a better idea of his capabilities. Although not remarkable, *The Last Supper* will bear comparison with contemporary works by the Flemish and Italian Masters. It is believed to be part of the series of five panels, which are on exhibition on the Ground Floor of the Prado, painted by Juan de Juanes for the Valencian Church of St. Esteban, later bought by King Charles IVth. *The Last Supper* was looted by the French during the Napoleonic invasion, but was returned to Spain in 1818, being valued at 250.000 «reales» in the Prado catalogue of 1834. At that period it was regarded as a masterpiece, but today is recognized as little more than a copy of the world-famous da Vinci fresco, though Juanes' St. John—his face alight with love as he gazes at Jesus—is a fine, and moving piece of original work.

The portrait of Don Luis de Castellá (for many years believed to be of Don Luis de Castelvi) was also bought in Valencia by King Charles IVth, and appears in the catalogue of the Royal collection in 1814. It is an interesting study, and suggests that Juan de Juanes might have been better advised if he had devoted himself to portrait painting instead of to the conventional religious themes of the period.

We now come to the first Spanish painter who was prepared to make portraiture his main interest—Alonso Sánchez Coello—disciple of the outstanding Dutch portrait painter, Antonio Moro, who paid three visits to Spain at the invitation of King Philip IInd. There are portraits of no less than four Kings by Coello on exhibition in the Prado. His work is accurate and careful and, although he never attempted to achieve Greco's uncanny penetration into the minds of his models, he is revealed as an acute observer with a fine sense of colour.

Madrazo said of Coello, «his work contains many of the best elements of the Flemish and Venetian Schools and, although he can never rival Titian, Raphael or Holbein, his portraits are well executed, and he makes use of a distinctive, though pleasing, range of cold tones to achieve his effects».

Coello's portrait of King Philip IInd in mourning is particularly interesting, and reveals the pale, fanatic face, compressed lips and keen, cold gaze—so strangely lacking in all sense of human kindness—that stamped this monarch's personality so strong-

ly upon his times. It was looted by the French during the Napoleonic invasion, but returned to Spain in 1816, entering the Prado 11 years later. For many years it was attributed to Coello's
pupil Pantoja. The canvases of the ill-fated Prince Charles and
Isabel Clara, painted in 1558 and 1579 respectively, are distinguished examples of Spanish portraiture before the genius of
Velázquez had created new world standards.

Coello's famous disciple, Juan Pantoja de la Cruz, never quite
achieved his Master's eminence, but there are two vigorous canvases by him, *St. Augustine* and *St. Nicholas de Tolentino*, which
reveal him an equal as a painter, even though lacking Coello's
mastery of design and form.

Both are signed and dated 1601. Originally in the Colegio de
Doña María de Aragón, they came to the Prado in 1933 from
the Museo de la Trinidad.

Francisco Ribalta, born in Spain's «Levante», and generally
regarded as a disciple of Juan de Juanes, has only recently been
given the attention that his work undoubtedly deserves.

Early in his career Ribalta decided to break away from the
fashion prevailing among his Spanish contemporaries, who were
still wholly under the influence of Raphael, and to return to a more
realistic style. It is true to say, therefore, that, although to a less
notable extent than El Greco, Ribalta was equally representative
of the transitional period, and so shares with the great Cretan the
credit for having laid the foundations for the masterpieces of the
16th. century—the Golden Age of Spanish Art.

In a recent book, Don Carlos Espresati says that Ribalta «felt
from the beginning the vital need to present the human figure in
true perspective, without the conventional tricks of vague outline
and half-tones popularized by the contemporary Roman School,
and to portray his models with brilliant realism, so that they stand
out unequivocally from their surroundings».

Ribalta has been accused of «tenebrism»—that love of obscure
backgrounds of which Caravaggio was the supreme exponent in
Italy—and of this Espresati remarks, «Tenebrism developed simultaneously in both Spain and Italy in a way that can only be

accounted for by the basic temperamental similarity that existed between the two artists».

Ribalta's *St. Francis of Assisi Comforted by Angelic Music* is strikingly realistic in its treatment though, in our opinion, his *Christ Embracing St. Bernard* is an even greater picture.

The latter was bought by the Prado in 1940, having been originally in the possession of the Carthusian Monastery of Porta Coeli, near Valencia. Until some fifty years age it was ascribed to Zurbarán, but is now known to have been a product of the last phase of Ribalta's life.

While much of Ribalta's best work is in Valencia this painting in oils is the equal of anything from his brush, both for its masterly sense of design and its sober employment of colour. The half-length figure of the saint—his face alight with divine love, and his right hand touching the arm of Jesus in a gesture of utter content—is intensely moving. The ivory coloured habit, and rosy flesh tints used in the painting of Our Lord, make it easy to understand how this picture was first mistaken for the work of Zurbarán.

The *St. Francis* was bought from the Capuchin monks of Valencia by King Charles IVth. in 1802, and appears in the first Prado catalogue. Its unpretentious naturalness has always been the object of favourable criticism, despite all changes in artistic taste.

The Dominican Friar, Juan Bautista Maino, was born in Milan, but is completely identified with the Spanish School of painting which immediately preceded the appearance of Velázquez. After many years of indifference to his work the critics of today greatly admire this artist. Perhaps the finest of Maino's canvases in the Prado is that portraying *The Recovery of Bahia in Brazil.* Employing clear tones, the group on the left of the picture is surprisingly modern in its conception, and the profile of a woman carrying her naked child in her arms, is beautifully executed. In 1701 this canvas was believed to be the work of a Flemish artist, and was valued at 120 «dobloons». Looted by Napoleon's brother Joseph, it returned to Spain in 1815, hanging first in the Academia de San Fernando and, in 1827, in the Prado.

The Adoration of the Magi by the same artist strikes us as being too vivid in its colouring but, if you can overlook this possible defect, it will be seen that both the Virgin and Child are beautifully portrayed. *The Adoration* came from the Museo de la Trinidad in 1873.

José de Ribera—«El Españoleto»—was born in Játiva, near Valencia, in 1591, but worked in Naples for most of his life. There are nine oil-paintings by him here, and others on the Second Floor. Although Ribera lived amid the brilliant light and shade of the Mediterranean he chose only dark tones and sombre themes for his work, following in the Caravaggio tradition of «tenebrism». One critic wrote that he «painted everything by the light of the wine-cellar», and it is true that a large part of his canvases appear to be covered by impenetrable shadows which, however, serve to heighten the dramatic contrast offered by the small area of intense light in which the main interest of the picture is centred.

Ribera's style was particularly admired in Spain, as it broke away from the old Italian and Flemish tradition and opened up new ideas and theories in technique for the younger Spanish artists of his day, paving the way for Zurbarán, Velázquez and many others.

The essential quality of Ribera's work can be appreciated in the two oil-paintings exhibited here—*The Martyrdom of St. Bartholomew* and *The Dream of Jacob*. Here the criticism which applies to almost all painters, except Greco and Fra Angelico, immediately strikes us—namely, the entire absence of religious feeling in the figures portrayed. Ribera's Saints reveal no spiritual exaltation, being nothing more than a faithful portrait of the model. The religious theme, in fact, again serves only as a pretext for painting, and the Saints can often be identified only by some conventional attribute or device.

The Martyrdom of St. Bartholomew is beautifully balanced and executed but, alas, the Saint is all too obviously a typical Italian fisherman. The strong bodies of the three executioners, however, are almost worthy of Michael Angelo in their muscular splendour. This canvas is less dark than many by Ribera, who signed it not only with his name but also with the word «Spanish», as he frequently liked to do. It was painted in 1640 and entered the Prado from the Royal collection. In 1794 it was valued at 60.000 «reales».

The Dream of Jacob, also signed, belongs to the previous year, and is an impressive example of Ribera's work, the face of Jacob, and the dream of the ladder itself, being admirable. When it was in the Elizabeth Farnesio collection it was ascribed to Murillo. It came to the Prado from the Academia de San Fernando in 1827.

Ribera made three canvases of *Mary Magdalene* (some believe of St. Thaïs) of which the one before us now is the best. Generally speaking Ribera was less successful in his portraits of women, but in this case the extraordinary beauty of the model—the same as was used for the *St. Agnes* in the Dresden Museum—is faithfully reproduced, and provides a striking contrast to contemporary Italian work which, by the early XVIIth. century, was already decadent.

Mary Magdalene was in the collection of the Marqués de los Llanos, before being catalogued in the new Royal Palace in Madrid in 1772.

Ribera's *The Trinity*, believed to have been painted in 1636, was bought for the Prado, in 1820 by King Ferdinand VIIth, from his own Court Painter, Agustin Esteve. A duplicate is still in El Escorial, and is particularly notable for the vigorous modelling of the body of Christ.

Opposite «El Españoleto's» pictures there are eight by Zurbarán, which naturally encourages comparison between these Spanish contemporaries.

Zurbarán's work was more placid than that of Ribera; his colouring clearer, and he does not share the latter's predilection for muscular nudes.

Zurbarán's reputation was at its lowest during the second half of the XIXth century and, now that he is valued more highly, the Prado has only an inadequate collection of his works. The two best—scenes from the life of St. Peter Nolasco—cannot be compared with those to be seen either in the Sevilla Gallery or in the Monastery of Guadalupe, and there is not a single example in the Prado of Zurbarán's famous series of portraits of monks, in which the artist's skill is most clearly revealed.

However, *The Visions of St. Peter Nolasco* and his *St. Casilda* are intensely Spanish in their sober and restrained treatment, perhaps even more so than the work of Velázquez, who travelled extensively in Italy whereas Zurbarán never left his native country and whose whole training and experience reflect his background. In any case the tendency to compare the two is unwise, as they should be judged separately on their own merits.

Enrique Lafuente Ferrari wrote, «Zurbarán reflects contemporary Spain to a remarkable degree. Unlike Ribera—who specialized in dramatic martyrdoms—Zurbarán clearly admired the aesthetic and contemplative heroism of the cloister and, probably for this reason, supplied much of his best work to the Spanish religious Orders. It seems probable that, like Velázquez, Zurbarán began his career with still-life pictures before he discovered his special vocation for religious painting. Although his name is Basque he was a typical product of Extremadura—«rustic yet austere».

Zurbarán was a master of design, and a good, sober colourist. When the theme required it, however, as in the figure of St. Casilda, he knew how to vary his tones, though he obviously preferred white, grey, black and clay-coloured reds. His blues tend to be too dark, and his use of green and ochre unattractive.

The two signed canvases, *Vision of St. Peter Nolasco*, in the Prado were painted in 1629 for the Sevillian Convent of the Merced Calzada. By the beginning of the XIXth. century they were in the possession of the Seville collector, López Cepero, who presented them to King Ferdinand VIIth. in exchange for a copy of a Velázquez portrait.

It is believed that the beautiful *St. Casilda* was painted for an altar, but it was mentioned in the 1814 inventory of the Royal Palace in Madrid, and came to the Prado five years later.

The signed, *St. Jacob de la Marca*, originally painted for the Chapel of St. Diego in Alcalá de Henares, was in the Museo de la Trinidad before it reached the Prado and, in 1933, was on exhibition in the Madrid Church of San Francisco el Grande.

St. Diego de Alcalá was formerly part of an altar-piece, and was presented to the Prado by Don Emilio de Sola in 1932. *St. Lucas Contemplating the Crucifix*, brought to the Prado in 1936, is interesting because of the theory that the figure of St. Lucas may have been a self-portrait of Zurbarán.

The still-life picture, catalogued as No. 2803, was a gift from the politician Don Francisco Cambó. It is ascribed to Zurbarán, though there are some doubts on the point. In any case it is a very fine example of that artist's style in treating a non-religious subject.

The Prado possesses 10 canvases by Zurbarán which are not on exhibition. These include six of the famous *Hercules* series, painted to decorate the Salon de Reinos in the Retiro Palace, and are among the best of the artist's known work.

It was not until quite recent times that Friar Juan Andres Rizi's portrait of Don Tiburcio de Redin y Cruzat was definitely identified. As late as 1818 it was catalogued in the Royal Palace at Aranjuez as a representation of Hernán Cortés by Velázquez. In 1819 it was listed as a *Portrait of an Unknown Gentleman,* by Mazo, and it was only Don Aureliano de Beruete who finally ended the uncertainty.

Technically speaking it is the equal of anything from the brush of Velázquez, and strongly recalls that artist's portrait of Pulido Pareja in the National Gallery in London.

This portrait, together with that of Friar Alonso de San Vitores in Burgos, are the two best-known examples of Rizi's work.

The name of Antonio de Pereda is not as well-known as it should be, judging by the quality of his three signed canvases now before us, two of them on religious themes and one on an historical subject, and all intended for the Retiro Palace.

The historical picture was looted by the French General Sebastiani, at the same time as several by Rubens, from the Convent of Loeches, and for many years was believed to have been lost. However, it appeared at a sale in London in 1912, when it was bought by the Hungarian collector, Marcel de Nemes, for the Prado.

In our opinion *St. Peter Freed by an Angel,* which was bought by the Prado in 1931 from the Count de Leyva, is a finer example of Pereda's work than his *St. Jerome,* and reveals the artist's unmistakable quality.

This section of the Gallery is completed by two portraits of French-born Queens of Spain. One is of Isabel de Valois, a copy

by Pantoja from the original by Sánchez Coello: the other, by
an unknown artist, of King Philip IVth's first wife, Isabel de
Bourbon.

HALLS XI, XII AND XIII

The Prado contains no less than 50 paintings by Velázquez,
including the best by the Sevillian Master. No other Gallery in
the world has such a collection, which includes examples from
every phase of his career.

Leaving out all works in which the hand of a pupil can
be detected, or concerning which there is the least possible doubt
as to authenticity, there are the following pictures by Velázquez
on exhibition here.

In Hall XI two *Crucifixions, The Adoration of the Magi*, portraits of Sister Jeronima de la Fuente, Don Diego de Corral, and
Doña Antonia de Ipeñarrieta, and two head and shoulders—one
of which is believed to be a self-portrait, and the other of the
painter Francisco Pacheco.

In Hall XII, *The Topers, The Spinners, The Surrender of
Breda, The Forge of Vulcan, Mercury and Argus*, the figures
of Aesop, Menipo and Mars, and 19 portraits. These last include
three of King Philip IVth and two of Prince Baltasar Carlos, besides those of the Princes Ferdinand and Charles, Queen Mariana
of Austria, the Princess Margarita, the Duke of Olivares, the 10th
Count of Benavente, the sculptor Martínez Montañés, the court
jesters and dwarfs Pablo de Valladolid, Barbarroja, Don Juan de
Austria, El Primo, Niño de Vallecas, Calabacillas and Don Sebastián de Morra. This hall also contains a landscape by Mazo, entitled
View of Saragossa, in which the figures in the foreground were
painted by Velázquez.

In Hall XIII there are the religious pictures, *St. Anthony the
Abbot with St. Paul the Hermit*, the *Coronation of the Virgin
Mary*, two small landscapes of the Villa Medici; four small portraits—two of King Philip IVth, one of the Infanta Maria, and
the other of Doña Juana Pacheco, wife of the painter—and
also a full length portrait of a clown, incorrectly entitled, *Don
Antonio el Inglés*.

Next to Hall XIII, dominated by the equestrian portrait of Isabel de Bourbon, is a corridor leading to the small room where *Las Meninas*—probably the most famous of all Velázquez's works—is exhibited alone.

In addition to the canvases already mentioned Halls XI and XII also contain the following pictures: a landscape attributed to Velázquez entitled *The Arch of Titus in Rome*, another landscape, two full-length portraits by Mazo, *Philip IVth and Mariana of Austria at Prayer*, a portrait of Prince Carlos, in which the hand of one of Velázquez's disciples can be detected; another portrait of Philip IVth, this time with a lion at his feet and, lastly, a portrait of the Duke of Pastrana by Carreño.

While the sculptor Rodin likened Velázquez to Phidias, there have been modern critics who expressed the opinion that he was too cold and academic to be considered really great. Such criticisms arise from the present day superficiality which, in its restless search for new forms of expression, cannot understand Velázquez's balanced harmony, proceeding from the serene and logical mind, possible only to his day and age.

In fact, Velázquez was the natural product of his times. By the end of the XVIth. century the artistic revival of the Italian Renaissance had spent itself, the place of the great Masters being occupied by decadent copyists of mediocre talent. Their last really valuable ideas were assimilated by Greco and transplanted by him to Spain, where they were developed along new and highly individualistic lines. At this psychological moment Velázquez appeared on the scene, and may be said to have written that last chapter in the book of Renaissance painting which the Venetians were unable to complete.

This final flowering of Renaissance Art was simultaneously reflected by Velázquez in Spain, and by Rembrandt, Van Dyck and Frans Hals in the Low Countries and, of these, Velázquez and Rembrandt are the supreme exponents. Velázquez was painting during the years when the baroque was in the ascendant, yet his work reveals no trace of its elaborate contortions. In fact, his delicate silver tones and deeper, but still subtle, browns and reds, supporting a design that deliberately eliminates all inessentials, contains the very essence of Andalusia transferred to the crisper air of Old Castile, the vigorous «chiaroscuro» of his youth gradually giving place to the delicate graduations of light and shade of his maturity.

Yet he is a supreme craftsman who masters every aspect of his art with brilliant certainty. True the early Velázquez is frankly experimental, but the mature artist is able to suggest a background of subtle light and shade never achieved by anyone else.

The three canvases in the Prado belonging to Velázquez's earliest Sevillian period, when the artist was about 20 years old, are *The Adoration of the Magi;* the portrait of Sister Jerónima de la Fuente, and that believed to be of Francisco Pacheco in Hall XI. All reveal something of Ribera's strange predilection for darkness, but as soon as he reached Madrid Velázquez became a favourite at Court, and developed his own special genius for portraiture.

Inevitably his rapid rise to fame attracted jealousy, and the King himself told him that his rivals accused him of being able to paint nothing but heads. While this accusation was profoundly untrue, Velázquez's interest was undoubtedly centred in the portrayal of the human face, and it was in this that he achieved his greatest triumphs, capturing character, individuality and temperament as very few others have ever succeeded in doing.

Even before he reached Madrid Velázquez had made himself a complete master of his art, as he demonstrated in the brilliant study of Sister Jerónima. However, after his arrival at Court, he developed still further his extraordinary ability to record the essential qualities of even the most unattractive models.

The only type of Velázquez's work that is not represented in the Prado is of the female nude, of which only a single example is known to exist, namely that on exhibition in London. Apart from this it is extremely rich in portraits illustrating every phase of his career, the only outstanding portraits by Velázquez which are not to be found in the Prado being those of Pope Innocent Xth, the Infanta María Teresa, Prince Philip Pospero and Juan de Pareja. The rest are all here: King Philip IVth. and his two Queens; the King's brothers, Ferdinand and Charles, and his sister María; The King's son and daughter, Baltasar Charles and Margarita; his minister the Duke of Olivares, and also of the King's numerous dwarfs and jesters. There are, additionally, the portraits of the

lawyer Don Diego de Corral; the sculptor Martínez Montañés; of
Ambrosio Spinola, and the Count of Benavente, and many others.
Besides these there are portraits believed to be of the artist's
wife; of his own Master, and a copy by Velázquez of a Góngora
head, which is in the possession of the Prado but not on exhibition.
Finally, there is Velázquez's own self-portrait in middle age, which
gazes back, serene but pensive, from the shadows of his masterpiece, *Las Meninas.*
The most notable of his works are now examined separately.

The Adoration of the Magi was painted in Seville in either
1619 or 1617, and is the earliest known work by Velázquez, who
must have been only 18 or 20 years old at the time. The Virgin
Mary is believed to have been a portrait of his wife, while his
father-in-law served as model for one of the Wise Men of the
East. Some critics have even suggested that the face of the youngest
is a self-portrait of the artist in his youth. This picture, when in
the Escorial collection, was ascribed to Zurbarán owing to the dark
background so characteristic of that artist.

The full-length portrait of Jerónima de la Fuente is signed
and dated 1620, but was only rediscovered as a genuine Velázquez in 1927, when it was shown in Madrid at a Franciscan
Art Exhibition. It came from the Convent of St. Isabel in Toledo,
and was bought for the Prado in 1944. There is a duplicate in
Madrid in the possession of Señor Fernández Araoz.

Next comes the portrait of Don Diego de Corral, Judge of
the Supreme Court of Castile, with his wife, Doña Antonia de
Ipeñarrieta and their small son, painted in Madrid in about 1631.
Incidentally, Don Diego was the only Judge who opposed the
imposition of the death sentence in the famous trial of Don Rodrigo Calderón. Some critics claim that the unconvincing treatment of the child suggests that it was not the exclusive work of
Velázquez. This canvas was the property of the Dukes of Villahermosa, and was patriotically presented to the Prado by the late
Duchess in 1905, after she had refused various large offers from
a foreign collector.
The chief point of interest in this picture is the head of Don

Diego, which reveals a perfection of technique not to be found elsewhere until a later period in the artist's life.

Velázquez's *Crucifixion* is of special interest because of its total absence of the traditional emphasis upon physical agony. In it the body does not seem to hang from the Cross but rather to rest upon it, and nowhere is the smooth flow of its majestic lines broken by the contortions that are the usual indication of suffering. The bowed head is hidden by the hair, and the body reveals its dreadful punishment only by the small wound in the side, and the thin threads of blood on hands and feet, and the whole impression, while intensely moving, is strangely serene and peaceful.

The Crucifixion was painted between 1632 and 1635 for the Madrid Convent of San Plácido, and came to the Prado in 1829. It became the joint property of the Infante Don Luis, the Countess of Chinchón and the Duke of San Fernando de Quiroga. The Countess took it with her to Paris where, in 1826, it was valued at 20.000 francs. However, the Spanish Government intervened to buy it for 30.000 «reales», but the Countess died before the sale was completed, and her heirs refused to be bound by the unratified agreement. Fortunately for Spain the Countess in her Will bequeathed the right to her brother-in-law, the Duke of San Fernando de Quiroga, to select for himself any one picture from her collection, and he chose Velázquez's *Crucifixion*, later presenting it to King Ferdinand VIIth. In 1834 it was valued at 120.000 «reales».

The story is that *The Crucifixion* was commissioned by King Philip IVth as a gift to the Convent of San Plácido in order to persuade the Abbess to permit him to visit a beautiful nun named Margarita, with whom he was passionately in love. The story rings true, from what we know of King Philip IVth. and of this particular convent, but Madrazo preferred to suggest that the picture was presented to the Convent by its Patron, Don Jerónimo de Villanueva.

There are many *Crucifixion* in the Prado painted by great Masters, but this by Velázquez is almost certainly the finest. Don Antonio Ponz, when he saw it late in the XVIIIth century, still in the possession of the Convent said, «It is the most powerful, yet delicate of studies, coloured with all the astonishing richness of Velázquez's palette».

The small sketch, *Christ on the Cross* may have been a preliminary design, for approval by the Convent of San Plácido, before Velázquez began work on his *Crucifixion*. It is particularly interesting for the fact that, although both signed and dated 1631, it was discovered only a few years ago in the Madrid Convent of the Bernardas del Sacramento. As a token of their gratitude for the rebuilding of their Convent, which was destroyed during the Civil War, the nuns then made a gift of the sketch to the Government, who presented it to the Prado in 1946. It was very unusual for Velázquez to sign his works—this sketch, and his portrait of the nun Jerónima de la Fuente, being the only examples of his signature among the 50 undisputed examples in the possession of the Prado.

Two early portraits—one of Francisco Pacheco and the other a possible self-portrait—reveal a vigorous «chiaroscuro» treatment, together with a wonderfully exact technique. The former, believed to have been painted in 1619, was catalogued among King Philip Vth's collection at La Granja in 1746. The supposed self-portrait is ascribed to the year 1622-1623, when the artist was a young man of 24.

It is generally agreed that the most important of Velázquez's works, belonging to the period between his arrival in Madrid and his first visit to Italy, is that known as *The Topers*.

In 1629 King Philip IVth paid the artist—who had already been appointed to the official position of Court Painter—the sum of 100 silver ducats for this canvas, and was so delighted with it that he forthwith decided to send Velázquez to Italy to complete his studies. *The Topers* appears in the catalogue of the old Alcazar Palace for the first time in 1636, the inventory of 1794 valuing it at 40.000 «reales», while that of only 40 years later estimated its price at no less than 180.000 «reales».

The theme of *The Topers* is vaguely mythological, and was at one time known as *The Triumph of Bacchus,* and represents a group of riotous wine-bibbers, wreathing themselves with vine leaves. It is a brilliant portrayal of the high spirits engendered by a drunken orgy, but the moral warning is present in the two faces looking directly out from the canvas, upon which the characteristics of the habitual drunkard are unmistakably stamped. A baroque painter, equally with a modern one, would have felt obliged, in treating such a theme, to include various unpleasant details in the interests of «realism», but Velázquez contrives to give a certain dream-like elegance even to a scene which, in its essence, is fundamentally vulgar.

The Topers probably reveals the culminating point in Velázquez's technical development before he left Spain. His subsequent contacts with the works of the great Italian Masters inevitably influenced the next period of his life when, with maturity added to experience, he was finally to establish himself as a painter of permanent world repute.

From the period of Velázquez's first visit to Rome the Prado possesses his *Vulcan's Forge*, the artist's treatment of which shows that he was far more interested in executing a number of studies of the male nude than in the theme that the title suggests, and Italian influences are more pronounced in this canvas than in any other. Painted in 1630, it was brought to Spain by the artist and, 4 years later, was presented by Don Jerónimo de Villanueva to the King. First catalogued in the Retiro Palace in 1701, it was valued at 80.000 «reales» in 1794, and at exactly double that sum in 1834. The theme, which is presented with a certain element of satire, shows the appearance of Apollo, determined to revenge himself upon Venus for her refusal of his love by denouncing to Vulcan the whole tale of her misconduct with Mars.

The Surrender of Breda commemorates Philip IVth's great victory, when the Genoese, Ambrosio Spinola, defeated the Dutch under Justin de Nassau. It was painted some time before April 1635, the capitulation itself having taken place 9 years earlier. Velázquez met Spinola during his first visit to Italy, but the Genoese leader had been dead for several years before the painting of *The Surrender of Breda*, as had also the Dutch leader, but the artist still contrived to present them both as vital, living personalities. The 30 spears or lances, appearing in the right upper section of the canvas, temporarily earned for it the title of *The Lances.* Incidentally, it is suggested that the soldier behind the horse on the extreme right may be a self-portrait of the artist.

In 1834 *The Surrender of Breda* was valued at two million «reales», and many people consider it the finest work of Velázquez's second period—1630 till 1649—and second only to *The Topers* among all that he painted before the age of 35, and it certainly provides a marked contrast to the crude colouring used in such early work as *The Adoration of the Magi.* In fact, the period of time which separated the painting of *The Adoration of the Magi* and *The Surrender of Breda* is 16 years, while that between *The Surrender of Breda* and another of his greatest works, *The Spinners* is 22 years.

The Spinners is believed to have been painted in 1657, that is to say, one year after Velázquez finished his supreme masterpiece *Las Meninas,* so that it is clear that this is the period in which the artist reached the summit of his powers. The room shown in the background is in the Madrid tapestry works of St. Isabel Street, and shows five of the workers engaged in their craft.

Originally the property of Don Pedro de Arce, Master of the Hunt at the Court of King Philip IVth, it was hung in the old Alcázar de Madrid, being damaged during the great fire of 1734. Removed to the Retiro, and thence to the new Royal Palace, it was valued at 60.000 «reales» in 1794. By 1834, having already reached the Prado, the estimate of its value had doubled but, even so, it was still, strangely enough, considered less than half as valuable as Juan de Juanes' *Last Supper.*

In *The Spinners*—as in *Las Meninas*—Velázquez clearly sought to interpret the very essence of light and shade, and those indefinable qualities of depth peculiar to an interior. In this he is the antithesis of the Flemish primitives. While, for example, the Master of Flémalle, in his *St. Barbara,* depicts every detail with meticulous care, Velázquez seems to see his subject through half-closed eyes, that record only the essential qualities of the individual and his surroundings. In some strange way he makes us feel that it is the background alone that lends significance to the human figures that he portrays.

It is often essential for a work of art to be seen from a

6

distance, and this is particularly true of Velázquez. From close
at hand it is possible to perceive only a series of heavy blobs of
colour yet, from the correct distance, these resolve themselves into
living human figures of an intense vitality. The extraordinary
subtlety of the artist is fully revealed by the fact that the most
arresting figure in the whole canvas is a young peasant girl, her
face hidden, barefoot and poorly dressed, whose only adornments
are the bright ribband in her hair and the simple bracelet on her
left wrist.

It is interesting to reflect that, in his 58th year, the Master
turned away from the recognized beauties of the Court, to the
portrayal of whom he had devoted the best part of his life, and
sought his inspiration among the simple people who had been his
models when he was a young and unknown artist in his native
Seville. In any case it cannot be denied that in these working
women of the Madrid tapestry factory Velázquez found the material
for his greatest works, and it was his representation of such simple
and unglamorous types, and in a setting devoid of all adornment,
that he finally demonstrated the range of his genius.

It is perhaps permissible to wonder how many masterpieces
have been lost through the failure of other artists to find this
inspiration in the every day people surrounding them. Most of the
great Masters of each century have devoted themselves exclusively
either to religious themes or to fashionable portraiture, but if,
instead, their brushes had recorded the colourful life of XVIth
and XVIIth. century Spain the world of today might be richer
by innumerable canvases such as «The Spinners».

Velázquez was the first to break away from convention, but
he did so only after he had recorded the decadent splendours of
the Court of *Philip the Great,* where Royalty was encouraged to
squander the hours of its youth in producing such elaborate coif-
fures as those shown in the portraits of Queen Mariana and the
Infanta Margarita.

Velázquez made several portraits of his patron the Duke of
Olivares, among them the equestrian one painted in 1634 which
is on exhibition here in Hall XII. It clearly reveals the strict ins-
tructions given by the Duke as to the way in which he wished to be
presented to posterity, and the result, as might be expected, lacks

something which the artist would otherwise have imparted to it.

From its original owner this somewhat idealized portrait passed into the possession of the Marqués de la Ensenada, being bought by King Charles IIIrd for 12.000 «reales» in 1769. After its entry into the Prado, in 1834, it was valued at 80.000 «reales».

The portrait of the Andalusian sculptor Martínez Montañés was formerly believed to be of Velázquez's friend Alonso Cano. Supposedly painted in 1637, when the sculptor visited Madrid to model a statue of King Philip, it was catalogued among the Royal collection at the Quinta del Duque del Arco and, in 1834, was valued at 10.000 «reales». Considered by many to be among the best of the Velázquez portraits in the Prado, the head and right hand reveal the artist's unmistakable technique. Strangely enough the left hand was never finished.

The half-length portrait of the Count of Benavente was in the collection of Elizabeth Farnese, where it was mistakenly ascribed to Titian. It came to the Prado in 1819, and was valued at 16.000 «reales» in 1834. The influence of Greco, as well as of Titian, are easily discernible, but both colour and design are in Velázquez's best vein.

This Hall contains various portraits of King Philip IVth. and his family, including Queen Mariana, the Infantes Don Charles and Don Ferdinand, Prince Balthasar Carlos, and the Infanta Margarita. The three of the King show Philip, first as a severe young man dressed in mourning and was painted in 1628; the second, on horseback, which is even earlier in date and was intended for the Salon de Reinos in the Retiro Palace; and the third, in hunting costume carrying a gun and with a sporting dog at his side, which is dated as between 1635 and 1638.

The equestrian portrait is additionally interesting as including by far the most successful representation of a horse ever achieved by Velázquez, whose animals were not, as a rule, very convincing. There is a charming group of King Philip, Don Fernando and Balthasar Carlos, believed to have been intended for the Royal Hunting Lodge at La Torre de la Parada in the Palacio del Pardo which, however, does not appear in the Catalogue until 1701. In

1834 those of the King and his son were valued at 40.000 and 25.000 «reales» respectively.

The three full-length portraits are made against a background of stormy sky and grey countryside, and are brilliantly executed, though it is the exquisite profile of the young Prince beneath his gaily coloured cap that most clearly reveals the hand of a Master. Velázquez painted several portraits of the young Heir to the Throne, who was to die before reaching manhood, of which this, and another on horseback, are to be seen in the Prado. This equestrian portrait was valued at 50.000 «reales» in 1834. The Prince's pony has been the object of much adverse criticism, and its preposterous barrel-like belly is surprising in the work of an artist usually so scrupulous in his attention to detail. One explanation of this improbable-looking steed is that Velázquez intended the portrait to be hung high above a certain door in the Palace, and seen thus from below its proportions are immediately restored to normal.

Although Velázquez's name is associated with the portraiture of royalty he never lost his interest in depicting the strange characters that helped to make up the Court of a XVIIth. century monarch. Among these were the macabre collection of clowns and dwarfs with which Philip IVth. liked to surround himself. To any one possessing the insight into character of a great portraitist it was clear that these figures of fun were anything but gay, and only one of the many inhabitants of this strange half-world painted by Velázquez is portrayed laughing. The exception is in the portrait of Calabacillas, and even here the idioti merriment so brilliantly portrayed moves us more to pity than to amusement.

Velázquez, in 10 portraits, reveals two distinct kinds of Court Jester, the clowns and the dwarfs. Among these there is a further division between the sane and the obviously cretin. Pablillos, Barbarroja and Don Juan de Austria appear to have been physically normal, while the dwarfs El Primo, Morra, Don Antonio el Inglés, Mari Bárbola and Nicolás Pertusato are at least sane. Clearly abnormal, both physically and mentally, are El Niño de Vallecas and Calabacillas. Incidentally, both the dwarfs Mari Bárbola and Nicolás Pertusato appear in the supreme Velázquez masterpiece, *Las Meninas*.

The artist's preference for full-length portraits of his models standing is clearly revealed, in that all this motley crew of Court Jesters are so presented. They were painted at various dates between 1633 and 1644; that of Pablo, being the earliest of the series, and that of Calabacillas, El Niño de Vallecas and Barbarroja dating from three years later. The richly coloured portrait of Don Sebastián de Morra is attributed to the year 1643 or 1644. Uncertainty surrounds the date when Velázquez made his portrait of Don Juan de Austria, and it is certain that the lunatic Don Antonio el Inglés had died in 1617, before the artist first left Seville.

All Velázquez's portraits of Philip IVth's Court Jesters were in the Royal collection, and those of Pablo de Valladolid, Barbarroja and Don Juan de Austria were in the San Fernando Academy from 1816 until 1827, when they were sent to the Prado. The first Prado Catalogue included those of Morra, Don Antonio el Inglés, El Primo, El Niño de Vallecas and Calabacillas. By 1834 each was valued at 20.000 «reales».

Which is the best of this strange set of portraits? Probably those of Don Juan de Austria and El Niño de Vallecas, the latter being a masterly study of character.

The Prado possesses two Velázquez portraits of Queen Mariana of Austria, the niece and second wife of King Philip IVth. One has been in the Louvre since 1941, as part of an exchange of works of art between France and Spain; the other and, in our opinion, the better, being catalogued Number 1191. Some critics believe that the canvas lent to the Louvre is only a copy of that now on exhibition in the Prado, though Señor Sánchez Cantón holds that they are duplicates, both by Velázquez, though that in Paris was the earlier, and painted from life. His view is supported by the greater freedom of style displayed in the Prado canvas. Although this portrait is not so fine as that of the Infanta Margarita, there is a striking similarity of treatment. Both mother and daughter are wearing the hooped skirts typical of the period, and are similarly coifed with a large feather head-dress, while both hold a white gauze handkerchief across their wide dresses.

Queen Mariana was an unattractive model, heavy and unintelligent, in marked contrast to her beautiful predecessor Isabel de Bourbon. It required all the Master's genius to make something of interest from the sullen expression and stiff artificiality of his subject, but somehow he overcame even these handicaps, and the result is technically brilliant.

This portrait belongs to the last period of Velázquez's life, being ascribed to the years 1652-53, and reached the Prado from El Escorial in 1845.

That of the Infanta Margarita is believed to have been Velázquez's last portrait, and some critics are of the opinion that it was finished by Mazo after the Master's death in 1660, and there are undoubtedly signs of another brush in the treatment of the model's face, neck and hands, as well as in the background, though the hair, dress and handkerchief are unmistakably by Velázquez.

The portrait of Queen Mariana is a study in black, silver-grey, pale red and ochre, while that of the Infanta is an equally marvellous symphony in red and silver, picked out with white and gold. Both reveal the supreme phase in the artist's development, his characteristic restraint in the use of heavy colour, and his inimitable delicacy of touch. The portrait of the Infanta Margarita came to the Prado in 1834, when it was valued at 30.000 «reales».

Velázquez's *Mercury and Argus* was painted between the years 1657 and 1659 as one of a series of mythological themes for the Mirror Salon in the old Alcázar de Madrid. Three were destroyed in the great fire of 1734—*Venus and Adonis, Apollo Chastizing a Satyr* and *Psyche and Cupid;* while *Mercury and Argus* reached the Prado in 1834, when it was valued at 30.000 «reales».

Modern critics consider it one of the less notable of Velázquez's canvases, being over-dark but, even so, it is a fine example of the artist's technique during the last years of his life.

Two figures by Velázquez, entitled *Aesop* and *Menipo,* which have been in the Prado since 1819, were painted in 1639 and 1640. Valued at 25.000 «reales» each in 1834, they were intended for the Torre de la Parada. They are impressions of the famous author of the fables, and the cynic philosopher Menipo—the expression of the latter being particularly clever.

The canvas, *View of Saragossa,* is catalogued as being by Velázquez and Mazo—the small figures in the foreground by the former, and the landscape by the latter.

Hall XIII also contains examples of Velázquez's work, though in his less interesting capacity as a painter of landscapes and religious themes.

The Coronation of the Virgin Mary, for example, finely depicts a beautiful girl, but both she and the figures by her side are far more human than divine. In short Velázquez, being by nature a genius of portraiture, always portrayed mythological or religious characters without any of the essential idealization of the human models he engaged. *The Coronation* is believed to have been painted about the year 1642 for the Queen's Chapel, reaching the Prado in 1819, and being valued, 15 years later, at 80.000 «reales».

Velázquez's fondness for painting landscapes is further revealed in the large canvas, *St. Anthony the Abbot and the Hermit St. Paul,* and by the two small sketches of the Villa Medici.

Although the theme of the former is of St. Anthony marvelling at the Raven which every day brought bread to the Hermit in his grotto it is, in fact, a large landscape, filled with rocks, trees, and distant mountains set against a clouded sky.

Velázquez's two sketches of the gardens of the Villa Medici in Rome immediately call to mind the «impressionists» of the late XIXth century. Formerly it was believed that these sketches belonged to the artist's first visit to Italy, but today the technique they reveal is taken as proof that they were painted during his second visit. They were both in the inventory of the Alcázar Palace made at the time of the death of King Philip IVth.

The portraits of Philip IVth's sister, Doña María de Austria, and that believed to be of Doña Juana Pacheco, are both fine pictures. The former was painted in Naples in 1630, but was still in Velázquez's studio when he died 30 years later, while the other, believed to have been painted two or three years later, was bought by Elizabeth Farnese. Since 1746 it has been catalogued as a *Portrait of the Artist's Wife.*

The head and shoulders portrait of King Philip IVth, numbered 1185, was painted during the last 5 years of the artist's life, and the King, already over 50, is shown in a plain black suit and starched ruff against a dark background. His calm, but haunted, heavy face and pale hair, are portrayed with all the impressive simplicity of which Velázquez was the master.

Some years ago there was a controversy as to whether or not the portrait of a dwarf, erroneously entitled *Don Antonio el Inglés,* was painted by Velázquez—Allende-Salazar asserting that it was from the brush of Carreño. The technique is strongly reminiscent of Velázquez, and the official Prado Catalogue continues to attribute it to him on the grounds that certain parts of the canvas are undeniably by the Master, while the name of his collaborator, if any, is not known.

> The exit from Hall XIII leads through a corridor, marked as Hall XIV, where there are 3 large, dark landscapes by Agüero. At the end of it, alone in Hall XV, is Velazquez's supreme masterpiece, *Las Meninas.*

HALL XV

The picture which is generally accepted as being Velázquez's greatest masterpiece is exhibited alone in this small hall, with a mirror on the opposite wall so that the visitor may appreciate its extraordinary depth and perspective with the heightened clarity sometimes provided more effectively by a reflection than by the reality itself. This is the world-famous *Las Meninas*—the Maids of Honour. Its setting is the studio of the official Court Painter, and it shows the King and Queen reflected in a mirror in the background, Velázquez himself at his easel, the little Princess Margarita, her two young Maids of Honour, two of the Court dwarfs and a dog. Behind the main group are two secondary figures, and also that of a man in the far background, framed in the doorway as though looking back at the moment of his departure.

Las Meninas was finished in 1656, four years before Velázquez's death, and was greatly appreciated by the King who, two years later, rewarded the artist with the Knighthood of Santiago. After Velázquez's death the Cross of the Order was painted on to the tunic of his self-portrait in *Las Meninas* at the personal order of the King. *Las Meninas* was saved from the 1734 fire which destroyed the old Alcázar de Madrid Palace, and the slight damage that it then received skilfully repaired by Don Juan García de

Miranda. In 1794 it was valued at 60.000 «reales» and, at the time of its entry into the Prado in 1834, at 40.000.

Most people agree that it was Velázquez's culminating triumph, and many believe that it is the greatest picture by any artist to be seen in the Prado. Unquestionably it is one of the finest in the entire world, if only for its almost uncanny mastery of interior lighting, and it aroused Gautier to write, «This is Nature itself imprisoned within the bounds of realism». Weisbach summed it up as «the image of a whole epoch, surpassing the boundaries of mere portraiture». As early as the XVIIth. century Lucca Giordano said of *Las Meninas,* «It is the very Theology of Painting».

It is of interest to recall that although the Dutch and Flemish schools had already produced masterly «interiors», they had never been successfully attempted anywhere else until the time of Velázquez.

The beautiful grouping of the figures leaves nothing to be desired, but the sense of life and movement, together with the technical mastery of colour and tone, combine to make us realise that we are in the presence of something that has been achieved very seldom in the history of art, seeming to invite us to join the courtier group that still awaits us there, living and moving, across the gulf of nearly 300 years.

The effect is not so much «impressionistic» as of a magically induced illusion, by which we are permitted briefly to share in the lives of the Royal Family, and the scope of Velázquez's genius can be very simply understood by comparing this courtly scene with his equally brilliant handling of the simple workers in *The Spinners.*

In *The Spinners* the interest is deliberately focussed upon one figure, but in *Las Meninas* this is not the case, the eye being equally attracted to four—the Maid of Honour, Doña María Agustina Sarmiento, the little Infanta, the second Maid of Honour, Doña Isabel de Velasco, and the dwarf Mari-Bárbola. But it is not long before it is drawn irresistibly to the artist's face, the graceful gesture of Nicolasito Pertusato, and to the sleeping dog on the right.

The painting of the dog particularly interested Lafuente Ferrari who wrote, «It is painted with great masses of colour, and with a faint halo framing its outline, the same device being noticable in the execution both of the dwarf's head and of the hands of the boy by his side».

Velázquez portrayed, as no one else could have done, the tragic dignity of King Philip IVth's decadent Court, shadowed by some occult foreknowledge that only one more King of the Austrian House would ascend the Throne of Spain—the great line of the Emperor Charles Vth. petering out in near-madness just 44 years after *Las Meninas* was painted.

FLEMISH PAINTERS

After having seen *Las Meninas,* and before returning to the Central Gallery, it is convenient to visit the eight halls containing over 160 pictures by Rubens, his pupils and copyists.

Peter Paul Rubens—the outstanding figure of XVIIth. century Flemish art—was born 22 years before Velázquez, that is to say in 1577. He visited Spain twice on official diplomatic missions, in 1603 and 1628, and on the second occasion is known to have met the young painter from Seville, going with him to look at some paintings.

Rubens was already at the height of his fame, but does not appear to have exerted any influence on the 29 year old Spaniard who, by this time, had already decided for himself the style he intended to pursue.

The huge canvas *The Adoration of the Magi,* with its brilliant colours, is typical of the work of Rubens, as are also his *Garden of Love, The Three Graces, Nymphs and Satyrs* and *The Judgment of Paris.* Additionally, there is the remarkably fine portrait of Mary of Medici, Queen of France and mother-in-law of the Spanish King Philip IVth.

Rubens is the supreme exponent of the Baroque, but reflexion makes it clear that all the works attributed to him in the world's art galleries could not possibly have been painted by one man alone, and reason suggests that often he acted as an artistic director to his disciples and pupils rather than as the actual painter. His studio was specially equipped for this kind of work, which was so well done that it is often impossible to be certain which sections of any canvas were the Master's own work, and which were painted, under his direction, by one or more of his collaborators.

However, in thirteen cases in the Prado collection, it has been possible definitely to identify his assistants, who are listed in the catalogue as having been Paul Bril, Van Dyck, Van Uden, Paul de Vos, Snyders (two) Jan Brueghel (three) and Van Tulden (four).

There are no less than 67 ascribed to Rubens alone, even though some of these also reveal the work of another hand, though in a less marked degree. There are also three copies by Rubens from the originals by Titian and Holbein.

There are works by Rubens in Halls XVI, XVIII, XIX, XX, XXII and XXIII, and also on the Ground Floor of the Prado. As the Flemish School was so very prolific in its output we shall confine ourselves here to a description of a few of the most important examples.

HALL XVI

This contains some canvases by Van Dyck, but is principally devoted to Rubens.

Religious themes, such as *The Adoration of the Magi* and *The Holy Family with St. Anne* alternate with mythological, and essentially pagan subjects like *Perseus and Andromeda, The Judgment of Paris, Diana and Calixto,* and the frankly erotic *Nymphs Pursued by Satyrs* or *Garden of Love* rub shoulders with *The Triumph of Catholicism, The Triumph of the Church* and *The Eucharist Triumphing over Idolatry.*

These «triumphs» belong to a series of 17 panels ordered from Rubens by the Infanta Isabel Clara Eugenia as designs for a tapestry for the Madrid Convent of Descalzas Reales. The artist completed the commission in 1628 for a fee of 30.000 florins. The «cartoons» for the tapestry to be manufactured in Flanders were completed simultaneously.

The panels were presented to Don Luis Méndez de Haro, and were bought for the Royal Collection in 1694 from his son.

Of the 8 possessed by the Prado the 3 best are to be seen in this Hall. Because of their relatively small size many people overlook them, though they are very well worth a more careful examination.

The Adoration of the Magi is impressive for its rich colouring as much as for its great size. Even in this theme Rubens was unable to restrain his predilection for painting massive or muscular nudes, and the first impression is that he gave more attention to the powerful figures carrying their gifts to the Child than to the Child Himself. It was painted for Antwerp Town Hall in 1609. Three years later it was presented to Don Rodrigo Calderón, as a reward to the Minister for his labours on behalf of Spain and, on his death, was bought by King Philip IVth. It is believed that Rubens added to the original canvas during his second visit to Spain in 1628.

The Holy Family seems almost too tranquil a subject to have appealed to such an enthusiastically pagan painter as Rubens, but his representation of the Child is most attractive, though his Virgin Mary is the conventional Flemish type, and totally lacking in any suggestion of spirituality.

The Master's vigorous style and warm colouring are unmistakably in evidence in this canvas, which came to the Prado from El Escorial in 1839, having been bought from the sale of its original owner, the Marqués del Carpio, at the end of the XVIIth century.

The Garden of Love was bought by King Philip IVth at the sale of Rubens' work which followed the artist's death in 1640. In this canvas all the pagan elements beloved by Rubens are present—languishing, if over-nourished, ladies; pink and equally plump Cupids; ardent and muscular males; playing fountains, arrows, flowers and wine—combining to produce a scene of slightly turgid gaiety unimaginable to any Spanish artist of the same period, but one which nevertheless strongly appealed to the sensuous Philip IVth.

It is believed that King Philip IVth. personally commissioned Rubens to paint his *Perseus and Andromeda* which, however, was unfinished at the artist's death. Fortunately, Jordaens completed the canvas in such a clever imitation of the Master's style that it is difficult to distinguish which part is by Rubens and which by his successor. The model for the nude figure of Andromeda was almost certainly Rubens' second wife Helena Fourment, who is also recognisable as Venus in another work of Rubens' later years, *The Judgment of Paris*. Philip's younger brother, the Cardinal, wrote of *The Judgment of Paris* to the King, «it is Rubens' best work, the only criticism being that the three goddesses seem to be excessively naked».

HALL XVII

Here is to be found Van Dyck's great canvas, *The Arrest of Jesus* together with the best of his portraits. The Prado possesses 7 Van Dycks based upon religious subjects, one on a mythological theme and 5 lesser works.

Van Dyck, who was a disciple of Rubens, is one of the outstanding portrait painters of the XVIIth. century, and his likeness of the Marchioness of Leganés rivals the work of his great contemporary Velázquez. He lacked Holbein's exactitude of design, but had a more controlled sense of line than Rubens, and his title to greatness is now generally admitted. Unfortunately the lack of English portraits in the Prado prevents us from tracing the tremendous influence that Van Dyck, as Court painter to King Charles Ist, of England, undoubtedly exercised upon the brilliant British portraitists of the XVIIIth. century, such as Gainsborough and Reynolds. The portrait of Doña Polisena Spinola, Marchioness of Leganés, daughter of the victor of the Battle of Breda, is believed to have been painted when the artist was only 25, and is a feat which even Velázquez could scarcely have achieved at so early an age. Already the artist's special talent for the portrayal of hands is fully revealed.

In the same Hall are two portraits of women and seven of men, including a self-portrait together with Van Dyck's friend Sir Endimion Porter. This oval canvas, which is considered one of his best, was the property of Elizabeth Farnesio, and was catalogued at the Palace of La Granja in 1750.

Other interesting portraits are those believed to be of the engraver Paul du Pont, the musician Jacob Gaultier, painted in 1635 and 1625 respectively; that of the armless painter Martin Rickaert, and of Count Henri de Bergh, finished in 1630.

Fromentin commented: «If we examine Van Dyck's portraits in detail we see that the Master is at his best in whatever aspect of his subject happened specially to interest him, such as an idle hand, the turn of a woman's wrist, or a slender be-ringed finger. His style owes nothing to the XVIth. century, belonging wholly to the new generation of the XVIIth. century, whose full development he never lived to see. He showed a greater interest in the textures of silk and steel and in the fashions of his day than can be found in any of Rubens' work though, like his Master, he is occasionally guilty of a rather showy and mannered style in his efforts to create an impression of richness. *The Arrest of Jesus* belongs to Van Dyck's earliest years. It was bought at the sale following the death of Rubens for 1.200 Florins.

HALL XVIII

This hall contains eight paintings by Jacob Jordaens, of which three are outstanding—a portrait group, a religious study, and the artist's rendering of a mythological theme. Additionally, there is a small sketch of exceptional interest to which we would like to draw attention.

The first picture, entitled *The Artist and his Family in a Garden,* is believed to have been painted in 1622, and shows us Jordaens, his wife, his daughter Elizabeth and a maid-servant. It was in the Royal Collection at Aranjuez in 1794.

The canvas known as *The Mystic Betrothal of St. Catherine of Alexandria* is believed by some critics not to be by Jordaens, but to be the work of Van Dyck and, when in the possession of Elizabeth Farnesio during the XVIIIth. century, it was ascribed to Rubens. It also came to the Prado from the Royal Palace at Aranjuez.

Meleager and Atalanta, catalogued at the same time as the other two already mentioned, is really two separate canvases painted at different periods of Jordaens life, though the junction was so skilfully made as to be invisible. The left half of the picture belongs unmistakably to the last period of the artist's life.

Lastly, there is the sketch mentioned above, showing the head and shoulders of three wandering minstrels, which some critics have attributed to Van Dyck.

Jordaens was a disciple of Rubens, but lacked the Master's powerful sense of drama. Reinach said of him, «Jordaens is a brilliant painter but lacking in taste, occasionally producing a rather ordinary imitation of Rubens».

The Prado contains none of Jordaens most typical canvases, though his *Meleager and Atalanta* gives a fair indication of his best style. His *St. Catherine*, though less brilliant, is technically remarkable, and his family group is beautifully composed and executed.

The sketch of the wandering minstrels seems completely modern in its vital realism.

HALL XIX

This is devoted to Rubens, Van Dyck and Brueghel, the three best canvases being Rubens' portraits of Mary of Medici and Anne of Austria and his famous work *The Three Graces*.

The Prado contains many representations of mythological themes from the brush of Rubens, mention having already been made of *The Judgment of Paris*, *Perseus and Andromeda*, *Diana and Calixto*, and *Atalanta and Meleager*. Now we are before his *Rape of Ganymede*, *Ceres and Two Nymphs* and *The Three Graces*. Later we shall be seeing his *Birth of the Milky Way*, *Diana the Huntress*, *The Banquet of Tereo*, *The Rape of Hipodemia*, *Mercury and Argus*, and *Achilles*. However, although so numerous, none is the equal of the three naked figures representing the Graces—that on the left, incidentally, being Rubens' wife Helena Fourment.

The Three Graces was painted during the last years of the artist's life, and was kept by his wife in her bedroom after his death, ultimately being bought by King Philip IVth. One critic judged it the supreme example of baroque painting, writing «Rubens has here given us his ideal of feminine beauty—fleshy, pagan, sensual and gay—as typified by his wife Helena, who is the arch-type of the Flemish Venus now to be seen in every major European art gallery». The same writer, Díez Canedo, adds, «it is no accident that there are so many examples of Rubens' painting of mythological themes in the Prado, as a number were directly commissioned to decorate the Torre de la Parada in El Pardo just outside Madrid, where Velázquez was also similarly engaged. While our rich heritage of Titian is due to Philip IInd., we must equally acknowledge our debt to Philip IVth. for his collection of Rubens. Yet, even as under Philip IInd. Spain was at her greatest, and Titian the supreme exponent of the art of his time, so both Rubens and Philip IVth. represented the last flowering of a vanishing age. From his early studies Rubens absorbed the best of the heritage left by the Italian Renaissance, and combined it with the essential elements found in the Flemish «primitives».

Mary de Medici is the best Rubens portrait in the Prado. Painted between 1622 and 1625 it was bought at the sale following his death in 1640. Also in the artist's best tradition is that of another Queen of France, the Spanish born, Anne of Austria, wife of Louis XIIIth.

HALL XX

Here is to be found Rubens' *Diana the Huntress, The Birth of the Milky Way*, and the *Banquet of Tereo*. The catalogue makes it clear that Diana's hounds were painted by Paul de Vos, and that the work of one or more collaborators is also clearly distinghishable in *The Birth of the Milky Way*.

The gloomy *Banquet of Tereo*, originally intended for the Torre de la Parada, reveals most of the faults for which Rubens' work has been criticized—the overcrowded design, the hastiness of execution, and the general air of what, in a writer, might be called «pot-boiling»—quite unworthy of an artist of his genuine greatness.

HALL XXI

Jan Brueghel de Velours, born 9 years before Rubens, is the dominant artist in this room. His theme is an allegorical study of the human senses, two large canvases illustrating sight and

Angel músico.   Ange musicien.
Angel musician.   Musizierender Engel.

La Virgen de la Rosa.   *La Vierge de la Rose.*
The Virgin of the Rose.   *Madonna mit der Rose.*

La Virgen, el Niño, un Santo y un Angel.
The Virgin, the Child, a Saint and an Angel.
La Vierge, l'Enfant, un Saint et un Ange.
Madonna mit Kind, Heiligen und Engel.

Noli me tangere.

San Sebastián.   *Saint Sébastien.*
St. Sebastian.   *Der heilige Sebastian.*

La Emperatriz Isabel de Portugal.
The Empress Elizabeth of Portugal.

L'Impératrice Isabelle du Portugal.
Isabella von Portugal

Mater Dolorosa.

TIZIANO

Venus recreándose con la música.   Vénus se récréant avec la musique.
Venus listening to music.   Venus und der Orgelspieler.

PALMA "EL VIEJO"

La Adoración de los Pastores.   L'Adoration des Bergers.
The adoration of the Shepherds.   Die Anbetung der Hirten.

La dama que descubre el seno.   *La dame qui découvre son sein.*
The lady baring her Bosom.   *Die Dame enthüllt ihren Busen.*

Venus y Adonis.   *Vénus et Adonis.*
Venus and Adonis.   *Venus und Adonis.*

Santo Domingo de Silos.

Santa Catalina.   Sainte Catherine.
Saint Catherine.   Heilige Katharina.

El bautismo de Cristo.   *Le baptême de Christ.*
The Baptism of Christ.   *Die Taufe Christi.*

La Resurrección (Fragmento).   *La Résurrection (Détail).*
The Resurrection (Detail).   *Die Auferstehung (Ausschnitt).*

Cristo con la cruz a cuestas.   *Le Christ portant la croix.*
Christ embracing the Cross.   *Christus trägt das Kreuz.*

scent, and five smaller ones of all the five physical senses. These form a series presented to King Philip IVth's younger brother, the Cardinal—Prince Don Fernando—in 1634 by the Duke of Pfalz-Neoburg. The Cardinal sold them to the Duke of Medina de las Torres who, in turn, presented them to the King in 1636.

To our taste the *Five Human Senses* appear cold and hopelessly overburdened with detail, but his studies of flowers and also some small landscapes, together with his canvas *The Country Wedding*, are all exquisite of their kind.

HALLS XXII AND XXIII

Here there are further examples of the rather showy Rubens School originating not only in Flanders, but also from the studios of the Master's Italian imitators. For the most part they do not merit more than a passing glance from the visitor, unless, of course, he is making a special study of the period.

In order to preserve the historical sequence which we have so far followed, we recommend the visitor to return to Hall XIII and the Gallery. In the connecting corridor he will pass four mythological works, two by Ribera representing the torments of Ixion and Ticio, and two by Titian on the punishments of Ticio and Sisifus. Additionally there are several pieces of sculptuary, and a copy of Lucca Giordano's «The Death of Absalom» by Corrado Giaquinto. The original is at the Royal Palace at Aranjuez, and served as the model for the Royal Madrid Tapestry Factory, which produced one of its finest works from it in 1760.

The two Ribera canvases form part of a series of four painted in 1632, of which the other two—*Sisifus* and *Tantalus*—have been lost. Before reaching Spain the *Ticio* was on exhibition in Amsterdam when, according to Palomino, it produced so profound an impression upon a certain young matron that it caused her «to miscarry of a monster». These large male figures are fine examples of Ribera's deep knowledge of anatomy, but those by Titian are dark and without great interest.

The central part of the Gallery forms a kind of «tribune» where there is a bust of Villanueva, the architect of the Prado. Below it is a tablet stating that, when the work of restoration

7

was completed on December 12th. 1927, it was dedicated as an exhibition of Spanish painting. Beneath this is a bronze bust of the Emperor Charles Vth. by Pompeo Leoni, flanked by the equestrian portraits of King Philip IIIrd. and his Queen, Margaret of Austria. These equestrian portraits were painted by an unknown artist for the Salon de Reinos in the Retiro Palace, and reveal signs of having been retouched by Velázquez.

Opposite, and on either side of the door leading to the Velázquez Hall, are portraits by Carreño of Queen Mariana, widow of King Philip IVth., and their son Charles IInd., destined to be the last the Austrian Kings of Spain. Beneath them are some obscure landscapes by Agüero.

CENTRAL GALLERY

SECTIONS XXVIII AND XXIX

Here there are 15 works by Murillo on exhibition, including two large canvases in the form of arches, portraying the foundation of the Church of Santa Maria Maggiore; three versions of the *Immaculate Conception,* one of which was the favourite of Napoleon's Marshal Soult; three child studies entitled *The Children of the Shell, St. John the Baptist,* and *The Good Shepherd;* his rendering of the religious themes, *St. Bernard's Vision of the Virgin Mary, The Descent of the Virgin to reward St. Ildefonso* and, finally, the half-length paintings *St. James the Apostle* and *The Virgin of the Rosary.* Additionally there is a portrait of an unknown man, and two landscapes of less importance.

Bartolomé Esteban Murillo was born in Seville in 1617, and, until recent times, enjoyed a reputation equal to that of his contemporary and fellow-townsman Velázquez. Today, owing to a change in taste, he is infinitely less admired than his great rival, but there are many who still consider his religious paintings unsurpassed. His most pitiless critics are the admirers of El Greco's «psychological» portraits who, not unnaturally, can see nothing of merit in Murillo's rich but conventional studies of nothing but the outward aspect of his subjects.

In our opinion Murillo is well worthy of study for his technical brilliance alone. The succession of rather sickly-sweet Virgins, blond angels and cherubic children may easily lead to his vigorous and finished workmanship being overlooked. While his brush delighted in soft, feminine, or childish forms, his presentation of them was always decisive.

It must be borne in mind that the themes which Murillo chose to paint required rich colouring and gentle personalities, but there is no lack of virility in the artist's handling of his subjects. Murillo's soft realism marks one of the highest points in Spanish art, his essentially Iberian style being enriched by a close study of Van Dyck, and he profoundly influenced the Sevillian School of the XVIIth. century, as can be seen not only in the Prado, but also, if the visitor wishes, in the Art Gallery of Seville. Many of Murillo's paintings now in the Prado were brought from his native Seville during the XVIIIth. century, and it is recorded that, when on a visit there in 1729, Queen Elizabeth Farnesio, who was an enthusiastic collector of Murillo's paintings, bought all she could find. Among her purchases now in the Prado are, *The Holy Family (del Pajarito), The Good Shepherd, St. John the Baptist, The Children of the Shell, The Crucifixion, St. Anne and the Virgin Mary, The Annunciation, St. Bernard's vision of the Virgin Mary, The Descent of the Virgin to reward St. Ildefonso, St. Francis of Padua, St. Jerome, Rebeca and Elicer, The Old Spinner, The Galician Woman* and an *Immaculate Conception*—this last catalogued No. 973.

Murillo's three child portraits exhibited here would alone be enough to establish his right to be considered a great painter, his treatment of the delicate flesh tints in his *Infant Christ* and *St. John* being exquisite, proving him Velázquez's equal at least in this respect, whatever his detractors may say of his over-idealization of smiling and beautiful children.

The two magnificent canvases depicting *The Foundation of the Church of St. Maria Maggiore* were painted in 1665 for the Seville Church of St. Maria the White, from whence they were looted by Marshal Soult for Napoleon's collection. However, it was returned to Spain in 1815, being in the Academia de San Fernando until it reached the Prado in 1901.

The Patrician's Dream is particularly fine, the two sleeping figures and the rich golden tones employed by the artist placing it among his best works.

The better of the *Immaculate Conceptions* is, in our opinion, that which also attracted the artistically rapacious Marshal Soult. It was painted for the Hospital de los Venerables Sacerdotes of Seville, from whence it was taken to France, for sale by its «owner» to the French Government for 615.300 francs in 1852, and was then on exhibition in the Louvre Gallery for 90 years, where its exquisite modelling and rich colouring attracted world interest.

The full-length portrait known as *The Knight of the Collar* was bought in 1941 by the Prado from the heirs of the collector Don Tomás de Veri, and belongs to the last phase of Murillo's life, when his genius as a portraitist was fully devoloped.

The preoccupation with religious themes of Spain's XVIth. and XVIIth. century painters seriously limited their development in other directions, and this applies especially to Murillo, whose realistic genius as a portraitist alone raises his religious pictures above the contemporary level.

Murillo's tendency to handle a religious subject as a «genre» painting is clearly revealed in *The Descent of the Virgin Mary to reward St. Ildefonso* and *St. Bernard's Vision of the Virgin Mary*, which compare with his *St. Thomas of Villanueva*, or *St. Anthony* and the *St. Elizabeth of Hungary* to be seen in Seville. These first two canvases have been in the Prado since its foundation, and in 1794 were valued at 7.000 «reales» each.

In the opinion of Madrazo both belong to Murillo's best period, which fell between 1665 and 1682.

> The remainder of the Central Gallery contains, on one side, various religious paintings by Claudio Coello and Mateo Cerezo, and a portrait by Francisco Rizi while, on the other, there are canvases by Herrera («el Mozo»), José Antolínez, Villavicencio and Cabezalero, and landscapes by Mazo and Velazquez.

The position of Claudio Coello in Spanish art, at a moment when foreign influences were particularly strong, is of special interest. Coello died at 51, and was the outstanding artist during the reign of the last of the Spanish Hapsburg Kings, Charles IInd. It is said that the arrival in Madrid of the Neapolitan artist Lucca Giordano in 1692 hastened his death.

The best of Coello's works in the Prado are his *Triumph of St. Augustin, Virgin and Child surrounded by Virtues and Saints,* and *Virgin and Child worshiped by St. Louis, King of France.* All three are signed, and the first two dated, respectively, 1664 and 1669. The third of those mentioned above belonged to the Marquess de la Ensenada, from whom it passed into the possession of King Charles IIIrd, before reaching the Prado in 1819.

The Triumph of St. Augustin was painted for the Augustin Monastery of Alcalá de Henares, and reached the Prado from the Museo de la Trinidad. It is a typical Spanish baroque triptych of the late XVIIth. century in which, however, can be traced the influences of Velázquez, Murillo and Rubens.

After the death of Velázquez Spanish art became more ornate, gradually degenerating into the over-complex, decorative style known as baroque. Pedro de Madrazo said of Claudio Coello, «He was a colourist in the tradition of Rubens and Veronese». We do not ourselves share the view that he successfully combined in himself the best of Cano's design, Murillo's use of colour and Velázquez's understanding of perspective, but he possessed a genuine quality of his own, more essentially Venetian than Flemish in its inspiration. He is notable, in a period of general Spanish decadence, as being the last Spanish artist in the great tradition until the emergence, nearly a century later, of the tremendous figure of Goya.

Mateo Cerezo, who died aged 40 in 1666, has had a number of canvases in the Prado since 1819, the best of which are his *Assumption;* the *Mystic Betrothal of St. Catherine,* dated 1660 and bought by King Ferdinand VIIth. in 1829, and *St. Augustin,* signed and dated 1663, which was bought by the Prado in 1926. While overshadowed by his contemporaries, in this golden age of Spanish art, he reveals a certain mastery in his handling of colour which suggests that, if he had lived longer, he might have achieved real greatness.

Another painter, who was more famous for the richness of his palette than for his accurate drawing, was José Antolínez. The Prado contains two of his altar-pieces, *The Immaculate Conception* and *Death of Mary Magdalene.* Both reveal how Titian still actively influenced the Madrilenian School of the late XVIIth. century.

The Immaculate Conception, signed and dated 1663, was bought by the Prado in 1931. *The Death of Mary Magdalene*—the better of the two in our opinion—was bought by King Ferdinand VIIth. in 1829 for 2.500 pesetas, under the impression that it was by Mateo Cerezo.

The *Scene from the Life of St. Francis,* attributed to Juan Martín Cabezalero (1633-1673) was painted for the Madrid Convent of St. Hermenegildo, and was one of the 50 Spanish pictures looted during the Napoleonic invasion. It reached the Prado from the Academia de San Fernando in 1911. Some critics assert that it is the work of Claudio Coello, while others attribute it to Carreño but, lacking decisive evidence, it is still officially listed as being by Cabezalero.

The Triumph of St. Hermenegildo, by the Sevilla artist Herrera (the younger), was originally the property of the Carmelite Order, from whom it was bought by King Ferdinand VIIth. for 10.000 «reales» in 1832.

Posterity does not endorse Herrera's high opinion of himself, and he is chiefly remembered as the spiteful rival of Coello, Cerezo, Antolínez and Cabezalero, though this particular canvas of his reveals an undoubted impressionistic talent.

Children at Play, by the Andalusian knight, Don Pedro Núñez de Villavicencio (1644-1700), is an attractive study, in the style of Murillo, of typical street urchins of the period. It is of special interest as a portrayal of life in the XVIIth. century, at a time when most other contemporary artists were more concerned with religious themes than with their own times. It was catalogued in the old Alcazar Palace of Madrid in 1686 though, at that time, it was a smaller canvas than that which is on exhibition today, being subsequently enlarged by Lucca Giordano. It is almost the only signed work by Villavicencio in existence, and so has a certain value apart from its obvious intrinsic worth.

Francisco Rizi (1608-1685) was the less well-known brother of Friar Juan, and the master of both José Antolínez and Claudio Coello. His *Portrait of an Artillery General* is inferior to Friar Juan's portrait of Don Tiburcio de Redin, but it possesses interest as a character study.

Portraits and landscapes by Juan Bautista del Mazo reveal why Velázquez's son-in-law was also his favourite pupil. His works, however, seem to suggest that he suffered from, rather than profited by, his close association with his great master, and his portraits are in so exact an imitation of Velázquez's style as often to make them indistinguishable. His rather dark landscape of the Royal Gardens at Aranjuez entitled *The Triton Fountain*—often ascribed to Velázquez—is notably better than similar works by Agüero, but its general obscurity is contrary to modern taste.

HALL XXXII

We are now in the presence of the last and, in the opinion of many, the greatest exponent of Spanish art, Don Francisco Goya y Lucientes.

The Prado contains the following canvases by Goya: two group portraits of Charles IVth. and his family; three equestrian portraits of Charles IVth, Queen María Luisa and General Palafox; nine full-length portraits of King Charles IIIrd, Charles IVth, Queen María Luisa, Ferdinand VIIth, the Marchioness of Villafranca, the Duke of Alba, General Urrutia, Doña Tadea Arias de Enríquez and of Cardinal Luis de Bourbon. There are also nine half-length portraits of Josefa and Francisco Bayeu (Goya's wife and brother-in-law), General Ricardos, King Charles IVth, Queen María Luisa, the Marchioness of Villafranca, the actor Máiquez, Don Manuel Silvela and Don Juan Muguiro. Additionally there are the head and shoulders self-portrait; another of Van der Gotten, and the two famous «majas»: the nude and the clothed. In this same Gallery there are also the scenes from the war against Napoleon, known as *The Fight in the Puerta del Sol,* and the terrifyingly realistic *Moncloa Executions.*

There are also no less than 45 canvases designed for the St. Barbara Tapestry Works; 14 more with the strange, haunted designs with which the artist chose to decorate his own home; three oval canvases representing Agriculture, Industry and Commerce; two landscapes entitled *La Pradera de San Isidro* and *La Ermita de San Isidro,* the *Crucifixion,* the *Holy Family;* the sketch *St. Justa and St. Rufina,* and three still-life studies.

Lastly, there are eight studies entitled, *The Milk-maid of Bordeaux*, *Blind Man's Buff*, *The Drunken Builder*, *The Cut-throat*, *The Bonfire*, *Majo with a Guitar*, *Un garrochista* and *The Exorcised One*, besides a «caprice» known as *The Colossus*.

It is a tremendous collection, and one from which it is possible to form a really comprehensive idea of the vital, many sided personality of Goya, though there is reason to suppose that it will be still further increased in the near future by legacies and purchases. Already it is the finest Goya exhibition in existence and, in our opinion, it would be better if nothing of a later date were permitted in the Prado, subsequent artists belonging elsewhere, since they play no part in the great pageant of European Art developing between the late XVth. and early XIXth. centuries.

Probably the most famous canvases by Goya in the Prado are *King Charles IVth. and his Family*, the two *Majas*, and his portrait of his brother-in-law Bayeu. The two religious paintings are of small interest.

Goya's designs for the Royal Tapestry Works only occasionally reveal the artist's authentic genius, as he was severely limited by the requirements of his employers. There are more of these to be seen on the Ground Floor of the Prado, to which we shall refer later.

When the Prado was restored, and partially rebuilt through the generosity of the Duchess of Parcent, in 1927, the circular hall at the end of the Central Gallery was intended for the exhibition of the best of Murillo's works, but it has actually been devoted to Goya's two «majas» and some of his most notable portraits.

Immediately facing the visitor upon entry is his *Charles IVth. and Family* while, flanking the door, are the world-famous *Naked Maja* and *Robed Maja*. Here there are also the equestrian portraits of King Charles IVth. and of Queen María Luisa, both of which appeared in the first Prado catalogue. Additionally, there are a number of other portraits, and some preliminary sketches for his masterpiece *King Charles IVth. and his Family*.

King Charles IVth. and his Family reveals Goya as a superb colourist, though the general composition of the picture is not particularly inspired. Nevertheless, it is considered one of the three greatest treasures in the possession of the Prado, the other two being Velázquez' *Las Meninas,* and Jordaens' *The Artist's Family.*

King Charles IVth. and his Family contains the portrait of 14 persons, if we include the little boy in arms, and a self-portrait of Goya himself in the background. It was painted in the Royal Palace at Aranjuez in 1800, and 39 years later entered the Prado, being then valued at 80.000 «reales». Unfortunately, the canvas is showing signs of deterioration.

The tendency to compare this with *Las Meninas* is hardly justified, Velázquez's masterpiece being technically the superior from almost every point of view.

Although Goya was more interested in portraying women than men the Prado does not contain a single female portrait by him in his best vein. Probably that of Doña Tadea Arias de Enríquez, with its fine grey tones and pale rose background, is the best to be seen here. It was presented to the Prado by the grandsons of Doña Tadea in 1896. Of the equestrian portraits that of Queen María Luisa is outstanding, and it is interesting to recall that only three «sittings» were required by the artist in order to complete it.

The half-length portrait of an unknown woman, catalogued No. 722, unfortunately shows clear signs of having been folded into four before it reached the Prado from the Museo de la Trinidad in 1816, 12 years before the artist's death.

Goya's signed head and shoulders self-portrait in oils also came to the Prado via the Museo de la Trinidad from its original owner, Don Román de la Huerta. There is a duplicate which, in our opinion, is the better of the two, to be seen in the Academia de San Fernando, dated 1815.

Goya himself considered his portrait of Manuel Silvela, painted during the years of the French occupation, to be one of his best, both in its colouring and design. It was bought by the Prado in 1931.

Of Goya's many paintings of «majas», the two on exhibition near the entrance to this hall are the most famous, perhaps because of the widely held belief that the model was the beautiful Duchess of Alba, and the legend that she was the artist's mistress. The two portraits are identical in pose, the sole difference being that one is nude and the other clothed. One popular explanation of the two versions of the same pose is that the Duke of Alba suddenly expressed a desire to see for himself exactly what kind of portrait of his wife the artist was painting. Strongly suspecting that the Duke would not approve of the nude study, which was already finished, Goya, working at top speed, completed the other, modestly robed one, just in time to satisfy the suspicious husband. The story is the more credible as Goya, en occasions, could work at almost unbelievable speed. Additionally, the head of the robed «maja» is obviously a copy from the other one, and the dress itself also shows signs of having been painted in haste.

However, the official catalogue discounts these romantic stories, and states that the Duchess of Alba was definitely not the model for either of these portraits.

The two «majas» were painted between 1797 and 1798 and, in 1808, were the property of Queen María Luisa's favourite and Minister Manuel Godoy, who also owned the only other Spanish female nude of which we have record, namely Velázquez's *Venus of the Mirror*. The naked «maja» was at one time in danger of being burned as indecent, but was hidden in the Academia de San Fernando, and entered the Prado in 1901.

Much has been written about Goya's «majas», from the technical as well as the romantic point of view. Señor Sotomayor has recently pointed out, with truth, that the head of the nude «maja» is badly set upon the shoulders. Generally speaking the nude is the more finished work of the two, the clothed figure revealing a quite different, and far more impressionistic, technique.

HALL XXXIII

The outstanding canvas in this small room is Goya's large portrait of General Urrutia, painted some time during the last decade of the XVIIIth. century. It was bought for 50.000 pesetas in 1896 at the sale of the collection of the Duke of Osuna, and is an example of the artist's best style.

HALL XXXIV

This hall contains some of Goya's less successful works, such as his *Crucifixion* and *Holy Family*, together with his superb portrait of Bayeu.

The group portrait of the Osuna family reveals not only the brilliance, but also the occasional carelessness to which Goya confesses in his writings, a carelessness which is particularly evident in his commissioned work, as opposed to his paintings of a subject of his own selection.

His portrait of his brother-in-law, Francisco Bayeu, was made in 1795—the year of his model's death—and there is another in the Valencia Art Gallery. This portrait was exhibited, unfinished, in the Academia de San Fernando in the following year and, in 1866, it was bought for 400 «escudos» on behalf of the Museo de la Trinidad. It reached the Prado in 1872. This particular canvas is often referred to as «a symphony in grey», and is accepted as one of Goya's finest portraits, even though it had to be completed from a self-portrait made by the dead artist.

Goya achieved his effects either with a rapid, and almost impressionistic simplicity or, alternatively, by a totally contrasting extreme attention to detail. This portrait of Bayeu, together with his naked «maja», are the most striking examples of his second technique.

The small *Pradera de San Isidro* was also bought from the Osuna collection in 1896, the price paid for this delightful example of Goya's art being 15.000 pesetas.

HALL XXXV

The Moncloa Executions is a picture of terrifying vividness. In our opinion this and *The Lances* are the two finest historical canvases in the Prado but, although they can thus be compared with each other, they clearly emphasize the essential difference between the two great artists. This lies in the fact that whereas Velázquez was content to record history, Goya was a propagandist, passionately concerned to convert the beholder to his own opinion as to the rights and wrongs of the events he records. Velázquez,

with the detachment of an historian, confines himself to depicting
the episode; Goya, on the other hand, violently expresses his
personal sympathy for the ragged and desperate people of Spain
in their seemingly hopeless struggle against the remorseless perfection of Napoleon's military machine. Something of the artist's
own hatred for the invaders has inspired his painting of the hud-
dled group of Spaniards, with their stark gestures of despair ex-
posed in a nightmare glare of light. To Goya the French executioners were devoid of all humanity, simply a line of faceless
uniformed figures, their heads crouched over the sights of their
rifles, and it is in the dramatic contrast between this inhuman line
of executioners and the passionate despair of their victims, that
the picture's greatness lies.

The canvas shows unmistakable signs of having been painted
at top speed, and in the white-heat of the artist's own intense
emotion. Its companion piece, depicting the attack by the Spanish
crowd upon some of Napoleon's coloured troops in the Puerta
del Sol, although fine, is less effective than *The Executions*, owing
to its confused design.

It is believed that Goya painted both these pictures in 1814,
when he was specially commissioned, for 1.500 «reales», to per-
petuate the heroic deeds of the rebellion against Napoleon. Both
came to the Prado, valued at 8.000 «reales», in 1834, and were
listed in the catalogue of 1872.

Goya painted from the heart, and he obviously disliked doing
the conventional Court portraits that were occasionally required
of him. Both the portraits of King Ferdinand VIIth.—and the same
may be said of that of General Palafox—are almost caricatures.
The personal contempt for the King which Goya undoubtedly felt,
is barely concealed, though his natural genius now and then
dominates his feelings, as can be seen in his drawing of the head
of Palafox, and again in the fine colouring employed in the figure
of Ferdinand.

HALL XXXVI

Here you may see the macabre paintings with which Goya
decorated the walls of his home between the years 1819 and 1823,
when the lonely and deaf old man was nearing the end of his

long life. They are oil-paintings, having been saved for posterity by Baron Emil d'Erlanger who, in 1873, bought Goya's old house and employed the expert, Don Salvador Martínez Cubells, to transpose these wall-drawings to canvas. It seems likely that if Baron d'Erlanger had not done this the paintings would have been totally destroyed by the action of time and neglect.

After exhibiting them in the 1878 Paris Universal Exhibition they were presented to the Spanish Government in 1881, and appeared in the Prado the following year.

The black fantasies that dominated this period of Goya's life do not appeal to the general public, though modern critics regard these sinister glimpses into a haunted mind as masterly, and have described them as the «culmination of the demoniac aspect of Goya's genius». It is difficult to realise that the hand that scored the harsh outlines to the «black paintings» was the same as that which wrought the silver tones in the portrait of Bayeu, and the repulsive figures in the «Witches' Sabbath» seem unimaginable from the artist responsible for the serene harmony of the portraits of Silvela or of Doña Tadea Arias.

CORRIDORS

The corridor which encircles the main Goya hall, and is numbered XXXI, contains a number of very fine pictures, including some by Goya's two brothers-in-law, Francisco and Ramón Bayeu. The work of Ramón is of no special merit, but Francisco Bayeu has been described as «the greatest figure in XVIIIth. century Spanish art, with the single exception of Goya himself».

Francisco Bayeu was powerfully influenced by Mengs and, as a result, strikes us as excessively conventional, but the Prado contains no less than 20 of his works—mostly sketches on religious themes—though all are not on exhibition. He was at his best as a portraitist, which makes it all the more regrettable that there is only a single example of this branch of Bayeu's art, namely that of his daughter Feliciana. Additionally, there are a number of his designs, or «cartoons», for the Madrid Tapestry Works.

The head and shoulders portrait of Feliciana Bayeu was, at one time, believed to have been painted by Goya—which alone is an indication of its real quality—and was left to the Prado by the artist Cristóbal Ferriz in 1912.

In this same passage-way are a number of canvases by the Valencian painter Mariano Salvador Maella, another follower of Mengs, but one possessed of even less talent than Bayeu.

Antonio Carnicero's curious picture *The Ascent of a Mont-golfier Balloon in Madrid,* painted at some date between 1780 and 1790, is interesting for the glimpse it provides us of contemporary fashions. It was bought for 3.000 pesetas at the 1896 auction of Osuna House.

There is a discreet *Portrait of an Unknown Lady* by the same artist, which formed part of the Bosch legacy to the Prado, which was also, for some time, ascribed to Goya.

The Prado contains many still-life pictures by Luis Eugenio Meléndez of which some are on exhibition here. Meléndez, who was sometimes called «the Spanish Chardin», usually initialled all his canvases, and those before us were painted at various dates during the late XVIIIth. century for the Royal Palace at Aranjuez. They are realistic and carefully executed, though uninspired.

Giovanni Domenico Tiepolo, who was in Madrid in 1772, painted a series of eight canvases for the Church of St. Philip Neri on the following themes; *The Garden of Gethsemane, The Scourging of Jesus, The Crown of Thorns, The Fall on the Road to Calvary, The casting of lots for Christ's Raiment, The Crucifixion, The Descent from the Cross,* and *The Burial of Christ.*

The predominant tones are of varying grey, but the composition reveals a certain mastery of design. Those on exhibition here are *The Fall, The Casting of Lots,* and *The Burial,* the other five of the series being on the 2nd Floor of the Prado. In our opinion, the series should not be divided up in this way, but be shown together as they formerly were in the Museo de la Trinidad.

Giovanni Domenico was the son of the famous decorator Giovanni Battista, of whose work we shall have something to say in reviewing the contents of the next hall.

HALL XXXIX

The Venetian, Giovanni Battista Tiepolo, who died in 1770, shares this hall with Luis Paret y Alcázar, born in the same year as Goya, and the Valencian portraitist Vicente López Portaña (1772-1850), who succeeded Goya as official painter to the Court of Spain.

Tiepolo spent the last eight years of his life in Spain, and several of the richly coloured ceilings in the Royal Palace in Madrid are his work. His oil-paintings in the Prado, however, cannot be compared with the fresco decorations, where his baroque technique had greater scope.

His best works here are the fragments transferred from the walls of the Church of St. Pascual in Aranjuez, painted in 1769. They were removed to make way for some much inferior work by Mengs.

The most notable examples of Tiepolo's art to be seen here are his *Annunciation, St. Pascual Baylon, St. Francis of Assisi,* and *Angel Bearing the Eucharist;* the first and third of which are signed.

The Annunciation first appears in the Prado catalogue of 1828, and the canvas *St. Francis* was discovered, rolled up and broken, as late as 1914. The outstanding merit of Tiepolo was his brilliant handling of colour, which clearly reveals his Venetian birth and training.

There are six signed pictures in the Prado by Luis Paret—two in this hall, and four more on the second floor—and all possess the same attractive sense of atmosphere, though perhaps his *King Charles IIIrd. Dining in State* is the most notable. The artist signed this with the quaint phrase, written in Greek characters, «Luis Paret, the son of his father and his mother, painted this». This canvas was for many years in Russia, and was bought in 1933 from funds bequeathed to the Prado by the Count of Cartagena. Paret's small *Masked Ball,* unknown until then, was bought with the same funds in 1944.

Luis Paret has received less attention from the critics than he deserves, being a gifted colourist who achieved many original effects. He was a man of great personal culture, and has sometimes been called «the Spanish Watteau». In the opinion of Lafuente Ferrari he is «the equal of the French Masters of the XVIIth. century, such as Saint-Aubin, Gravelot or Cochin».

Probably because he was able to travel widely throughout Europe Paret managed to avoid the mannerisms of the period, and his small groups of figures, dominated by his special shades of blue, are often exquisite.

The Valencian Court painter, Vicente López Portaña, has a number of not very remarkable portraits on exhibition here, and also a fresco, painted in 1818 for the ceiling of the small palace, known as the *Casino de la Reina*, that was presented by the city of Madrid to King Ferdinand VIIth's second wife, Isabella de Braganza. It was sent to the Prado in 1865.

López was an excellent designer, but tended to overburden his canvases with detail. However, unlike such great portraitists as Holbein and Dürer, who also delighted in detail, the Spanish painter reveals no corresponding perception of character, preferring to model his style on Mengs rather than Goya. His ten portraits on exhibition here reveal him as little more than a painstaking artisan, whose whole talent seems to have been devoted to the portrayal of clothes, lace, feathers and embroidery, rather than to the human subject of the portraits.

The best of his works, in our opinion, is his portrait of Goya, in which there are indications that his model intervened to prevent López's excessive attention to detail. However, that of Queen María Cristina de Bourbon—and particularly her dress—is not unpleasing, though the dual portrait of Don Antonio Ugarte and his wife seems to us unattractive, both in colour and design.

Retrato de un santiaguista.   *Portrait d'un " santiaguista ".*
Portrait of an " santiaguista ".   *Bildnis eines " santiaguista ".*

La Trinidad.   La Trinité.
The Trinity.   Die Dreifaltigkeit.

ZURBARAN

Visión de S. Pedro Nolasco.
Vision of St. Peter Nolasco.

Vision de Saint Pierre Nolasco.
Vision des San Pedro Nolasco.

VELAZQUEZ

Los borrachos.   Les ivrognes.
The Topers.   Die Trinker.

VELAZQUEZ

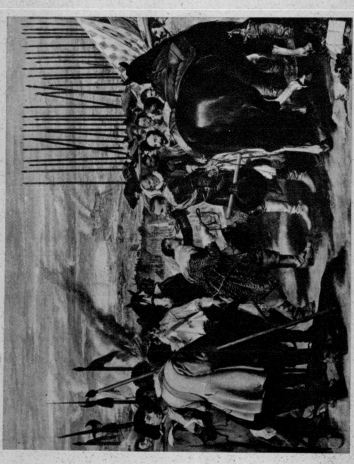

La rendición de Breda. *La reddition de Breda.*
The Surrender of Breda. *Die Übergabe von Breda.*

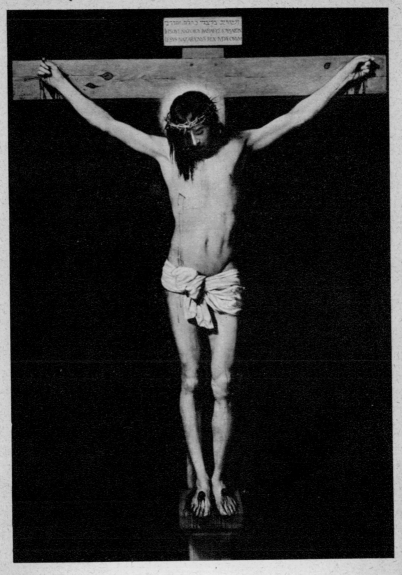

Cristo crucificado.   Le Christ crucifié.
Christ on the Cross.   Christus am Kreuz.

La Reina Isabel de Borbón.
The Queen Elizabeth of Bourbon.
La Reine Isabelle de Bourbon.
Königin Isabella von Bourbon.

S. Pedro libertado por un ángel.
St. Peter liberated by an angel.

Saint Pierre libéré par un ange.
Sankt Petrus von einen Engel befreit.

Retrato de Iwanowitz.   *Portrait d'Iwanowitz.*
Portrait of Iwanowitz.   *Bildnis von Iwanowitz.*

La Inmaculada Concepción "de Soult".
The Soult's Immaculate Conception.

Immaculée Conception "de Soult".
Die unbefleckte Empfängnis von "Soult".

El triunfo de San Hermenegildo.   *Le triomphe de Saint Herménégilde.*
The Triumph of St. Hermenegildo.   *Der Triumph von San Hermenegildo.*

La Asunción.   *L'Assomption.*
The Assumption.   *Die Himmelfahrt.*

El tránsito de la Magdalena.   *La mort de la Madeleine.*
The Death of Mary Magdalene.   *Der Tod Maria Magdalenas.*

GOYA

La maja desnuda.

GOYA

La familia de Carlos IV.   *La famille de Charles IV.*
The Family of Charles IV.   Die Familie Karls des IV.

GOYA

La gallina ciega.

GROUND FLOOR

If we enter the Ground Floor of the Prado by the North door, we find ourselves in a circular vestibule where there are a number of battle scenes painted by Snayers (1592-1667?). On the left there is a small hall, artificially illuminated, containing an extremely interesting fresco brought here from the Segovian village of Maderuelo.

This unique fresco was painted by an unknown Spanish artist of the XIIth. century. It was removed from the Hermitage of Maderuelo, where it was in danger of being entirely lost and, although some fragments are lacking, it is now well preserved against further deterioration.

The two main themes displayed over the entrance door are *The Creation of Adam* and *Original Sin*, both painted with the extreme simplicity of this very early period. The Segovian fresco has greatly enriched the Prado's collection of early Spanish art, and it forms an interesting introduction to the study of succeeding centuries, of which the building contains so many splendid examples.

> After seeing the Maderuelo fresco visitors are advised to enter the hall devoted to Spanish retable paintings, which is to be found at the end of the rotunda, where there is also specially designed artificial lighting.

HALL L

Here there is a small, but representative, collection of Spanish Gothic painting, including the earliest works in the possession of the Prado.

8

Impartial study reveals that although XVth. century Spanish painting is of real interest, it cannot be compared with contemporary Flemish work, which had mastered the art of oil-painting to a degree that was not achieved in Spain for another century and a half.

Two retables, each portraying three figures, and a number of fragments from others, are now before us. The first is the work of an unknown Castilian artist, and is called the *Retable of Don Sancho de Rojas* after the Archbishop who commissioned it for the Monastery of St. Benito el Real. It was bought by the Prado in 1929.

The second, dedicated to the Virgin Mary and St. Francis of Assisi, was bought one year later. It was originally found in a farmhouse near the village of La Bañeza, and is the work of Nicolás Francés who died in 1468. Both are of great beauty, though inferior to other panels to be seen here, such as *St. John the Baptist and St. Catherine* which came from the Los Arcos Chapel in Sigüenza Cathedral. This, together with four others belonging to the same group, is the work of the unknown artist called the Master of Sigüenza, at some date between 1430 and 1450, and was bought by the Prado in 1930.

In our opinion, there is no example of Spanish primitive painting to equal this panel, either for its brilliant colouring or for the serene beauty of St. Catherine.

Among the other panels on exhibition here the fine colouring of Pedro García de Benabarre's *Martyrdom of Saints Sebastian and Policarpo* should not be overlooked. Pedro García was born in the village of Benabarre early in the XVth. century. There is another retable signed by him to be seen in the Barcelona Gallery.

The two panels portraying *The Transference of the Body of St. James the Elder* came from a Church near Lérida, and formed part of the Bosch legacy. The artist is unknown, though he is believed to have belonged to the Aragonese School of the early XVth. century. Both are in a good state of preservation, and reveal the same remarkable vividness of colour.

In the opinion of one critic the author of the full-length panel *St. Vincent*, known as the Master of Archbishop Dalmau de Mur, is entitled to be named «the greatest of the Aragonese Masters of the mid-fifteenth century», and the extraordinary realism, finish and the advanced technique certainly merit the claim that he be considered «the Aragonese Jaime Huguet». *St. Vincent* came to the Prado in 1920 from the Madrid Archaeological Museum, in whose possession it had been since it reached the capital from Saragossa in 1871.

There is a small *Head of a Prophet* by Jaime Huguet which, though finely painted, is not the equal of those by the same XIVth. century Catalán painter to be seen in Barcelona.

The panels illustrating *The Story of St. Michael,* ascribed to the Master of Arguis, also came from their original village Church, reaching the Prado via the Archaeological Museum. The Master of Arguis is another early XVth. century Aragonese painter, his work being particularly notable for what has been described as its «narrative easiness».

> In order to preserve the essential sequence in time it is now necessary to cross the hall devoted to French painting, and make for the main western vestibule, numbered XLVII, and enter that devoted to sculptury, which is situated immediately below Velázquez's hall. On the right there is a door leading to nine halls, numbered LIX to LXVII, which are devoted to Dutch and Flemish painting of the XVth., XVIth. and XVIIth. centuries. Incidentally, all these nine halls, with their large eastern windows and fire-proof walls, were only inaugurated in 1942.

HALL LIX

This is devoted to Flemish and German artists of the first half of the XVIth. century.

The outstanding Flemish painter of the period was Ambrosious Benson, represented by seven panels illustrating religious themes. The German Christopher Amberger has two portraits on exhibition, believed to be of the goldsmith Jörg Zörer and his wife, which reveal the characteristics of the «primitive» German school. Both portraits were catalogued in La Granja Palace in 1746.

Benson's panels originally formed part of the retable of Santa Cruz in Segovia, and reached the Prado from the Museo de la Trinidad.

The collection, as a whole, does not compare with the best Flemish work of the XVth. century.

Pieter Coecke Van Aelst's triptych, *The Adoration of the Magi*, is in no way outstanding and, in our opinion, the head and shoulders entitled *The Saviour*, ascribed to Jan Massys, or Metsys—son of the more famous Quentin Metsys—is far superior, as are also Van Oostsanen's *St. Jerome*, the *St. Francis* by one of Van Orley's disciples, and the *Figure of Zachary* by Jan Prevost.

HALL LX

Here there are 15 portraits by Anthony Moor; the remarkable, *The Money Changer and his Wife*, by Marinus Claeszon van Reymerswaele—a legacy from the Duke of Tarifa in 1934—and the really beautiful *Portrait of a Humanist* by Jan van Scorel, bought by the Prado in the following year.

The Money Changer and his Wife, signed and dated 1539, is a brilliant character study, showing the acute concentration upon both faces, while their hands are counting the money before them.

The Dutchman Moor—known in this country as Moro—is considered the founder of Spanish portrait painting, and here we may study some of his best works. Outstanding are four portraits of women, the artist's wife Metgen, painted in 1554; that of Mary Tudor of England, wife and aunt of King Philip IInd. of Spain; thirdly, that of the wife of the Emperor Maximilian IInd., María of Austria, dated 1551 and, lastly, of Mary Tudor's intimate friend the Duchess of Feria, which belongs to a later period.

Additionally, there are full-length studies of the Emperor Maximilian IInd, and of the Court Jester Pejeron, both of which fully display Anthony Moor's remarkable genius.

The fact that he is more interested in the drawing, than in the colouring of his pictures reveals Moor's northern origin. He does not attempt the minuteness of detail typical of his great contemporary Holbein (the Younger), but his work is both vigorous and penetrating.

Some critics have failed to give Moor his just share of praise, Reinach not even mentioning him in his *Apollo*, but it is now generally admitted that no history of portrait painting in Europe is complete without some reference to him.

Probably the best single example of Moor's art is his portrait of his wife Metgen, with a richer colouring and lighter finish than is usual with him. A close second choice would be that of Mary Tudor, painted in the year of her marriage with King Philip, eleven years her junior. The Emperor Charles Vth. liked it so much that, when he retired to die in the Monastery of Yuste, he took it with him.

HALL LXI

The most notable canvases to be seen here are two hunting scenes by Paul de Vos, and two still-life studies by Peter Boel.

The Deer Hunt and *Deer pursued by Hounds* are both dated. These sanguinary struggles between animals are not to everyone's taste, but we must recognise the skill with which the artist contrived to suggest the speed and effort of the chase.

Peter Boel's two studies of fish, poultry, fruit and vegetables are in the best tradition of this speciality of Flemish art.

There are two excellent head and shoulder portraits by Justus Susterman in the Rubens style. They are of Mary of Austria, Grand Duchess of Tuscany, and the Grand Duke Ferdinand IInd. Also worthy of note is Peter Snayers' *The Cavalry Engagement*, dated 1646, and later bought by King Charles IVth.

On the other hand, *Immaculate Conception*, by Erasmus Quellyn, seems lacking in all real quality. It was a gift from the Marquess of Leganés to King Philip IVth.

HALL LXII

There is little to detain the visitor in this hall, though he will be rewarded by a glance at the expressive faces portrayed in Theodor Rombout's *The Dentist*, once in the Royal collection.

Boel's canvas *Game and Hounds* reveals technical ability, and *The Fruit Dish* by Frans Snyders is also a finished performance.

HALL LXIII

This contains the best Dutch paintings possessed by the Prado, with works by Rembrandt, Gabriel Metsu, Adriaen van Ostade, Hobbema, Gerard van Honthorts, Grebber, Wouverman and Schalcken.

Rembrandt's *Artemis, Queen of Pergamo*—though doubt exists as to the model's identity—is signed and dated 1634, when the artist was only 28 years old. Some critics believe that the face is that of Rembrandt's beautiful wife Saskia, of whom he painted several portraits. First the property of the Marquess de la Ensenada, it was bought for 2.500 «reales» by King Charles IIIrd. in 1769. It is generally considered the best of Rembrandt's early works, and the ash-blonde hair, the pale hands and rich dress, backed by the vase in which, tradition asserts, the Leyden artist's ashes were presented to the Queen, is all in the Master's finest manner. There is also here Rembrandt's famous self-portrait, made when he was about 55 years old, which was bought by the Prado in 1944.

The four small signed oil-paintings by Van Ostade were bought by Charles IVth., and reveal the King's excellent taste.

Gabriel Metsu's *The Dead Cock*, also bought by King Charles IVth. is remarkable for its exquisite finish and detail, and the landscape by Hobbema, bought by the Prado in 1944, posssesses a certain poetic quality. Van Honthorst's *Doubting Thomas* is not one of the artist's best works.

HALL LXIV

The outstanding pictures in this hall are the following: several still-life studies by Adriaensen; three by Clara Peeters which are, however, rather cold and mannered; two interiors of Flemish Churches by Peeter Neefs (the Elder); twelve small copper-plate etchings by David Teniers (the Elder); *The Gamblers* by Romboust; one by Snyders; a panel by David Ryckaert entitled *The Alchemist,* and forty small copper-plates by Van Kessel (the Elder), once the property of Joseph Bonaparte and presented to the Prado in 1865 by Count Hugo. These copper-plates represent different animals, and are assembled in the form of a triptych.

HALL LXV

This is chiefly devoted to David Teniers (1610-1690) famous for his lively crowd scenes. Among the best are his *Temptation of St. Anthony, The Surgical Operation, Country Dance, The Kitchen, Pipe Smokers and Drunkards, The Alchemist, The Graceful Kitchen-maid, Country Fair, The Gay Old Man, The Pipe Smokers, The Feast of the Villagers,* and *Le Roi Boit.* All of these, though small in size, possess a golden warmth, and show us simple folk making merry in XVIIth. century Flanders.

David Teniers broke away from the tradition of painting little besides altar-pieces and religious themes, and devoted his whole energies to portraying the rich and placid life that surrounded him. Though not considered a really great artist, there is no doubt that his work portraying the customs of simple people will live because of its sincere originality.

This gallery also contains Teniers' documental, rather tham artistic, portrait *The Archduke Leopold William in his Picture Gallery in Brussels,* which is signed, and dated 1647. It belonged to the collection of King Philip IVth.

There are a number of studies of dogs by Paul de Vos and Snyders of no especial value.

HALL LXVI

The six animal studies by Frans Snyders strike most people as unpleasant, their indifferent taste being particularly marked in his *The Fox and the Cat, The Table* and *The Hunted Boar.*

The two large canvases by Van Utrecht, a still-life study, and *Filopemenes Discovered,* are of a higher order than anything else exhibited here by Snyders.

HALL LXVII

Although there are some interesting works by Van Dyck, it is undoubtedly his master Rubens who dominates this hall.

Here we may see the most powerful of all Rubens' religious paintings, which is called *Piety*. It belongs to the artist's last epoch, and was bought by King Philip IVth. From El Escorial it came to the Prado in 1837. The face of Christ is of a moving nobility, and the drawing of His naked body is masterly.

Rubens' baroque style is fully revealed in the equestrian portraits of King Philip IInd. and, even more so, in that of the Cardinal Prince Ferdinand, younger brother of Philip IVth. and is strongly marked in the dynamic figure of *St. George* in his *St. George and the Dragon*.

Also to be seen here are Rubens' half-length portraits of the Infanta Isabel Clara and her husband, the Archduke Albert, and the *St. Austin Meditating on the Trinity* which is ascribed to him, but which some critics believe to have been by another hand.

In our opinion, Van Dyck's *Crown of Thorns* is a greater picture than his *Arrest of Jesus*, to which reference has already been made, and is probably his best religious work in the Prado. The rich and shining colours, and masterly sense of design, leave no doubt in the mind of the beholder that this is a great picture. Van Dyck presented it to Rubens and, at the sale following the latter's death, it was bought by King Philip IVth., reaching the Prado in 1839 from El Escorial. The Berlin Art Museum possesses a duplicate, which contains certain minor differences from the canvas now before us.

Hall LXVII leads into a corridor bearing the number LXVIII, but its contents are of little interest. The visitor may descend a few stairs to Hall LXIX, but here, too, the Flemish pictures, and collection of sculptury and tapestry are unworthy of prolonged examination.

The alternative corridor, numbered LXX, contains a large canvas by an unknown Flemish painter of the XVIIth. century, entitled «The Beheading of St. John the Baptist», and also the

«Neumaquia Romana» by Lanfranco; a «Holy Family» by Vicencio Carducho, and two panels by Juan de Juanes on the theme of «The Martyrdom of St. Stephen», of which the other three of the series are on exhibition in Hall LXXXV.

The visitor is advised to pass on to Hall LXXII, where there are seven portraits of the Spanish branch of the Royal House of Austria by Sánchez Coello, Pantoja and Villandrando. Here also are fifteen studies of flowers by Arellano and Bartolomé Pérez; statues of the Emperor Charles Vth. and the Empress Elizabeth; four reliefs and, inside a show-case, the collection of medals and ancient coins bequeathed to the Prado under the Bosch legacy.

The small Halls LXXI and LXXII contain, respectively, some interesting sculptury, including the famous pre-Roman «Lady of Elche» and, in five show-cases, the collection known as «The Dauphin's Treasure», of which we shall later have something to say.

From Hall LXXII the visitor passes the circular room numbered LXXIV, containing Spanish XVIIth. century pictures, and enters Hall LXXV, which is devoted to Spanish art of the XVth. and XVIth. centuries. Hall LXXIV contains two examples of the work of Valdés Leal and Claudio Coello, and one by Alonso Cano. The circular Hall LXXIV also exhibits paintings by the Master of Sisla, Alejo Fernández, Morales, Correa, Navarrete, Sánchez Coello, Masip, Juan de Juanes, Becerra, and others.

HALL LXXIV

Two undistinguished works by Valdés Leal—a *St. Jerome* and a figure of a martyr—are on exhibition here, and there are two more on the second floor, to which we shall refer in due course.

In order to appreciate Valdés Leal's work it is necessary to visit Seville, and it is interesting to recall that this artist, in his day, was considered a serious rival to the great Murillo, of whom he was violently jealous.

His *St. Jerome* reveals attractive brush-work spoiled by faulty design. Both this and *The Martyr* were painted for the Seville Church of St. Isabel, and were looted by the French during the Napoleonic wars. *St. Jerome* came to the Prado from Agnew House in London, in 1936, and *The Martyr* from the Madrid antiquary Sánchez Villalba in the previous year.

Claudio Coello's *St. Domingo de Guzmán,* and *St. Rosa of Lima* are good examples of the sober Spanish style of the XVIIth.

century. They are believed to have been commissioned for a Madrid Church before entering the Museo de la Trinidad, from whence they came to the Prado.

The Miracle of the Well, by Alonso Cano, represents an episode in the life of St. Isidro, and came into the possession of the Prado in 1941. The origin and history of this picture are unknown, but we shall have more to say of Cano when visiting the Second Floor.

HALL LXXII

This hall contains some interesting portraits, including a canvas by Sánchez Coello of King Philip IInd.'s two daughters, Isabel Clara and Catalina Micaela.

There are also portraits of Elizabeth of Valois; and of King Philip IInd. and Margaret of Austria, by Juan Pantoja, whose work we have already seen. The style is similar to that of Coello, and possesses the same preoccupation with the model's clothes, rather than his character, typical of all Spanish portrait painters before Velázquez.

Rodrigo de Villandrando's portraits of King Philip IVth. and his first Queen are similar in treatment, but inferior in quality, to those of Pantoja.

The collection of paintings of flowers, shown against a dark background, by Juan de Arellano and Bartolomé Pérez, hardly require special comment, beyond the recognition that they are faithful copies from nature.

HALL LXXV (GALLERY)

It is easy to see that Sánchez Coello was a far better portraitist than he was as a painter of religious themes. His *Betrothal of St. Catherine,* signed and dated 1578, additionally reveals a deplorable confusion between St. Catherine of Siena and St. Catherine of Alexandria. It was sold by the artist for 150 ducats, and was in the Escorial until 1839. Coello's *San Sebastián,* signed and dated 1582, came to the Prado from the Madrid Church of San Jerónimo el Real.

The supposed self-portrait, with something of the technical freedom of Titian, is a fine work, and was bought by the Prado in 1926.

Over a century ago the Museo de la Trinidad obtained six religious pictures by an unknown painter, known as the Master of La Sisla, from the Monastery of la Sisla, near Toledo, and these came into the possession of the Prado in 1872. The two most interesting are the *Adoration of the Magi*, and the *Death of the Virgin Mary*, believed to have been painted between 1480 and 1520.

The Prado contains three panels by Vicente Juan Masip, two circular and one oval. These are *The Visitation, The Martyrdom of St. Agnes* and *The Coronation of the Virgin Mary*, which were bought for the Prado by King Ferdinand VIIth. the circular panels for 9.000 «reales» in 1826, and the oval one, two years later, for 3.000. They were catalogued, until 1920, as being by Juan de Juanes.

The best, in our opinion, is *The Martyrdom of St. Agnes*, which closely resembles the work of Raphael, though *The Visitation* is only a shade less remarkable. The figures of St. Agnes and her executioner are finely portrayed, without any of the over-dramatization from which such a subject might easily suffer.

Juan Correa de Vivar was a little known Castilian painter of the XVIth. century. Although not a great master he was one of the best exponents of the Italian style that was so strongly influencing Spanish art at that period. His work resembles that of Juan de Juanes, though it also contains certain similarities with his contemporary Morales (1500-1586).

Of the eight pictures by Correa in the Prado the finest is undoubtedly his *Death of the Virgin Mary*. Painted for the Church of El Tránsito in Toledo it came here from the Museo de la Trinidad in 1872. It possesses an effective sense of restraint, combined with excellent design.

We must now draw the visitor's attention to the two versions of *Virgin and Child*, numbered 944 and 2655; the portrait of

Beato Juan de Ribera, and the *Annunciation* and the *Presentation of the Infant Jesus* by Luis de Morales.

Morales belongs to his period, which is that of the religious panel revealing both Italian and Flemish influences. Although his modelling is occasionally effeminate his best works show both a sincere religious feeling and a subtle perception of human emotion, which entitle him to be considered the best Spanish painter of the XVth. century, with the exception of El Greco.

His *Virgin and Child*, which formed part of the Bosch legacy, is generally considered the best work of its kind by Morales. A critic wrote on this subject, «Apart from its own extraordinary artistic merit this masterpiece is of particular interest as revealing the profound influence of the Renaissance upon Morales. The harmonious design and the finely drawn hands, so obviously copied from life, show that, although himself a disciple of a northern Master, Morales was profoundly influenced by Raphael or Michael Angelo, whom he sought to imitate».

The Beato Ribera portrait, for which it is believed that the venerable Juan de Villegas served as model, was presented to the Prado in 1896 by Doña María Enríquez de Valdés. The pale face, vibrant with personality, is beautifully executed. *The Presentation of the Infant Jesus*, bought by King Charles IVth., is also vivid with colour and movement, the best figure being that of the young girl passing before the Child and carrying a lighted candle. On the other hand, the figure of Jesus appears out of proportion, and the grouping is over-crowded.

The small picture *The Baptism of Christ* by Navarrete (the Dumb) was the means of introducing the artist's application for employment to King Philip IInd. This finely coloured and finished work was originally in El Escorial, coming to the Prado from the Academia de San Fernando in 1827.

FRENCH PAINTERS

The Prado does not contain anything like so representative a collection of French painting as it has of Spanish, Italian and Flemish masters. Those that it does contain, by Poussin, Watteau and Claude de Lorraine, not to mention lesser artists, will not bear comparison with the pictures to be seen here from the other three great Schools.

However, works by French artists are on exhibition in the large Hall LXIX, and the two small Halls LIII and LIV, as well as in the corridor numbered XLVIII.

Señor Sánchez Canton, who has written a small guide book to the French pictures in the Prado, claims that they are the least frequented of any in the building, and adds, «This may be because French classical art was under the influence of Rome and Bologna, whereas the Spanish school were inspired by the far greater Flemish and Venetian painters. French artists were primarily concerned with faithfully portraying their subject, while the Spanish are more interested in depicting the human emotions». «French painters favoured mythological themes, at a time when this kind of work was unknown in Spain, and they also specialized in landscapes in which the centre of interest was some man-made building, while in Spain they were concerned only with untouched nature. Similarly, while Spanish portraiture was essentially sober and realistic, that of France was frankly superficial. Again, the manner with which the artists of the two countries treated religious subjects is fundamentally different.»

«To understand French painting, therefore, it is necessary to realize that it belonged to another fashion and style, in which the artist's objectives were accuracy of design, the balance of the composition as a whole, the display of classical erudition and refinement, and the presentation of erotic themes.

HALL XLIX (GALLERY)

Known as the Bronze Hall, the pictures on exhibition here are mostly portraits of no very great merit.

Those of Louis XVIth. of France; Philip Vth. of Spain; Marie Theresa of Austria, wife of Louis XIVth. of France; Queen Christina of Sweden; Louise Elizabeth of Orleans; the Great Dauphin, father of Philip Vth. of Spain; Philip of Orleans, grandson of Louis XIIIth. of France; Victor Amadeo IInd, Duke of Savoy, and his wife and daughter Anne Marie of Orleans and

Marie Adelaide, all suffer from the artificiality typical of the
French Court painters of the period. The same criticism applies to
those of the Duchess of Montpensier and the Duchess of Bourbon,
and of the Royal mistresses Madame Pompadour and Madame du
Barry. It is believed that the equestrian portrait of Christina of
Sweden, by Sebastian Bourdon, was sent by the Queen as a gift
to King Philip IVth. in 1656. Although somewhat showy, it
reveals a certain mastery of technique. The portrait of Louis XVIth.
by Antoine Callet is in the approved manner for display in a
Royal Gallery, and was a gift from the tragic French King to the
Count of Aranda. It gives the unfortunate impression that Louis'
corpulent figure was only, with difficulty, restrained within the
bonds of his magnificent clothes!

The virtue of Jean Ranc's portrait of Louise Elizabeth of
Orleans lies in the fact that it was never finished, and thus escaped
the burden of fussy detail which was the besetting vice of French
art of the period. Ranc himself did not appreciate the fact, as he
remarks in one of his letters that the merit of his work lay precis-
ely in «les finir extraordinairement».

The portrait of *The Great Dauphin*, and his *St. Juanito*,
reveal Pierre Mignard as the superior of most of his French
contemporaries but, easily the outstanding work on exhibition
here is that of the musician Grétry, by an unknown artist. It was
part of the Bosch legacy to the Prado, and was at one time
attributed to Greuze. There is, however, a genuine Greuze, head and
shoulders of an unknown lady, bequeathed to the Prado in 1935
by Don José Brunetti, Duke of Arcos.

The corridor linking Hall XLIX with Hall LIII contains four
gloomy landscapes by Claude de Lorraine. There are also two
canvases by Michel Ange Houasse, who was employed in Spain by
King Philip Vth. These are entitled *Bacchanal*, which is dated
1719, and *The Sacrifice of Bacchus*, belonging to the following
year. Although they strike us as over-academic, and lack the verve
of Titian's *Bacchanals*, they reveal a pleasing harmony of line,
and deserve to be placed in a better light.

HALL LIII

Any visitor entering this Hall will be immediately struck by the large canvas entitled *The Family of King Philip Vth.*, which was painted in 1743 by Louis Michel Van Loo.

Despite its faults this picture is interesting as providing a typical example of French art of the period, and in demonstrating the influences at work upon Spanish painting in the lean years before the emergence of Goya. To understand how complete was this period of decadence in Spanish art, it is only necessary to compare Van Loo's *The Family of King Philip Vth.*, and Velázquez's *Las Meninas*, separated in time by only 87 years, but by a whole age in terms of quality. The simplicity, dignity and genuine greatness of Velázquez's art had been replaced by the cold superficiality, the affected conventionality, of such as Van Loo.

Designed to occupy the wall of a Royal Palace, its pictorial merits satisfied the limited artistic requirements of the period, and it is perhaps unfair to compare its slick, studied, and fundamentally false elegance with the work of the giants of the preceeding century.

Placed upon an easel opposite Van Loo's *Family of King Philip Vth.* is a delicately coloured portrait of Louis Ist. at about the age of 10. He was to be King of Spain for a few months in 1724 during a stormy interlude in the reign of his father, Philip Vth. It is ascribed to Houasse (1680-1730), who lived in Madrid for some years, and was clearly influenced by Velázquez.

The portrait of Louis XIVth. the Roi-Soleil of France, is by Hyacinthe Rigaud, and displays the usual preoccupation of the French Court Painters of the period, namely to please their sovereign rather than to achieve a great work of art. Showy and conventional, it presents Louis XIVth. as he wished to be remembered by posterity, rather than as a human being.

Rigaud (1659-1743) painted this portrait during the first decade of the XVIIIth. century, and it belonged to Louis' grandson, King Philip Vth. of Spain, entering the Prado in 1827. It is believed that the background is by Parrocel.

HALL LIV

The French artist Nicolas Poussin was a contemporary of Velázquez, and it has been said of him that he was to the art of his times much what Racine was to its literature. Both were classicists rather than classic: learned lovers of the antique, studious, but uninspired; interested in the form, but politely ignorant of the spiritual substance of what they were portraying.

Poussin is the supreme example of the academic neo-classicism of the period. Trained in Rome and inspired by Raphael, his two dark canvases, *The Bacchanal* and *Parnassus*, painted at the same time as Velázquez's *The Topers*, give a very fair idea of his capabilities.

Sánchez Cantón, writing of these two pictures says, «*The Parnassus* is inspired by Raphael's Vatican Stanzie fresco, into which he has introduced certain baroque elements. The nude figure of Castalia is the main difference between the two, while the ghosts flying among the trees reveal the influence of Titian. Calliope, the Muse crowning the Poet, is simply a copy of Minerva, without the usual helmet and spear. The other conventional figures shown are presumably intended to portray Dante, Petrarch and Aristotle on the right, and Homer, Virgil and Horace on the left. The colouring, particularly the yellows and blues, is more attractive than was usually the case with Poussin».

He continues, «*The Bacchanal* reveals the «*Philosopher Painter*» in a rather more inspirational vein, and is superior to the Bacchanals ordered by Cardinal Richelieu. It shows Bacchus inviting Ariadne and Cupid to mount his panther-drawn carriage. Before them goes Silenus, mounted on an ass, and various dancing bacchantes. The best group is that on the right of the canvas, showing a naked and drunken bacchante, riding a deer and supported by a satyr and a goat-footed child».

In our opinion Poussin's *Meleager's Hunting Party* is the best picture by the French master in the possession of the Prado. His *St. Cecilia*, also on exhibition here, belongs to the same period

Santa Bárbara (Fragmento).   Sainte Barbe (Détail).
Saint Barbara (Detail).   Heilige Barbara (Fragment).

Descanso en la huida a Egipto.
The Rest on the Flight into Egypt.

Le Repos dans la Fuite en Egypte.
Rast auf der Flucht nach Aegypten

La Virgen con el Niño.   *La Vierge avec l'Enfant.*
Virgin and Child.   *Maria mit dem Kinde.*

Las tentaciones de S. Antonio.   *Les Tentations de Saint Antoine.*
The Temptations of St. Anthony.   *Die Versuchungen des Heil. Antonius.*

El carro de heno (tabla central).   *Le Chariot de foin (Panneau principal).*
The Chaff Cart (Centre).   *Der Heuwagen (Haupttafel).*

PATINIR

Paisaje con San Jerónimo.   Paysage avec Saint Jérôme.
Landscape with St. Jerome.   Landschaft mit St. Jeronimus.

VAN HEMESEN

El cirujano.   Le chirurgien.
The surgeon.   Der Chirurg.

La Reina Maria de Médicis.   *La Reine Marie de Médicis.*
The Queen Mary of Medici.   *Königin Maria von Medici.*

Las tres Gracias.   Les trois Grâces.
The Three Graces.   Die drei Grazien.

RUBENS

Danza de aldeanos. *Danse des paysans.*
The dance of peasants. *Der Bauerntanz.*

JORDAENS

Meleagro y Atalanta.   Méléagre et Atalante.
Meleager and Atalante.   Meleager und Atalante.

La coronación de espinas.   *Le couronnement d'épines.*
Crown of Thorns.   *Die Dornenkrönung.*

Artemisa.   *Artémise.*
Artemis.   *Artemis.*

El Rey Felipe V de España. *Le Roi Philippe V d'Espagne.*
The King Philip V of Spain. *König Philipp der V von Spanien.*

Grupo llamado "de San Ildefonso" (Cástor y Pólux (?).)

La Dama de Elche.

as the other three paintings by him specially mentioned and completes a representative collection of his work.

The exquisite French painter Antoine Watteau died when he was only 37, but was the dominating figure among the contemporary school composed of Poussin, Le Brun, Fragonard, Claude de Lorraine and the landscape painter Claude Gellée. There are two oil-paintings by Watteau in this hall, entitled *Country Dance* and *The Gallant Feast*, which were once in the Elizabeth Farnesio collection. They are excellent examples of the «boudoir» pictures which portray life during this greatest century of French history.

The French paintings on exhibition in the Prado reveal flawless taste, marred by a certain aristocratic, academic coldness. Always correct, well-balanced, and designed to please the refined elegance of their patrons, it is, nevertheless, an art which seems a little insipid when compared with the deeper, more vital works of the Flemish, Venetian or Spanish schools.

HALLS LV, LVI AND LVII

These three halls were decorated in 1928, in the style of a XVIIth. century palace, for the exhibition of Goya's «cartoons», or designs for tapestries, and contain furniture appropriate to the period. The canvases, in their attractive gilded frames, are not hung, but are placed leaning against the walls. Their total of forty-one includes nearly all the designs ever made by Goya for the Royal Tapestry Works of Santa Bárbara.

In a book by Cruzada Villaamil, published in 1870, on the subject of these designs, the author lists 45, from which 92 tapestries, worth 600.000 «reales», were woven, Goya himself receiving 189.000 «reales» for the work.

The present Prado catalogue also lists a total of 45, though only 38 of these were mentioned by Cruzada Villaamil, the other seven having been discovered or identified since 1870. Among these latter are the first and last of a not particularly interesting series of eleven, begun by Goya before the year 1776 and terminated in 1791, which are entitled, respectively, *Picnic on the Banks of the River Manzanares* and *Blind Man's Buff*. Goya was

9

just 30 when Mengs recommended him for the post as one of the
artists who designed the tapestries for the Royal Factory, which
had been established half a century earlier. He began work there
in 1776 and, to begin with, his designs are few and of no outstanding merit. However, the opportunity afforded him invaluable
experience in the composition of canvases that ultimately captured,
as no other artist has ever done, the dances, picnics, plays and
bull-fights that together went to make up life in Madrid during the
last quarter of the XVIIIth. century. As such they represent not
only a welcome break with the old style preoccupation for mythological, religious or historic themes, but also afford us an invaluable and vivid glimpse of the period.

Goya's tapestries were made to decorate Royal Palaces, but
his designs reveal that his absorbing interest was in the common
people. He was passionately attached to his work, and contrived
to leave the mark of his special genius upon every one of his
designs. He delivered no less than 24 of the total of 45 exhibited
here during the years 1777, 1778 and 1779: four belong to the
year 1786, another four to 1787, two to 1788 and three to 1791.
All are oil-paintings upon a red-tinted linen cloth, which has tended to darken with the passage of time more than might have
been wished.

Some of these «cartoons» are the earliest of Goya's works in
the possession of the Prado.

For his *Picnic on the Banks of the Manzanares* he was paid
7.000 «reales» and, for *The Dance*, 8.000. For *The Quarrel, The
Maja and the Hooded Man, The Wine Bibbers*, and *The Parasol*,
all delivered to the Tapestry Works during the course of the year
1777, he received a total of 17.000 «reales». *The Picnic* is not the
equal of either *The Dance* or *The Maja and the Hooded Man*,
and the three painted during 1778—*The Blind Guitar Player, The
Fiesta of Madrid* and *The Crockery Seller*—are particularly fine.
Among Goya's work completed during 1786 mention must be
made of *The Vintage*—in our opinion the best of the series—*The
Flower Sellers*, and *The Injured Builder*. In the same vein are
The Snowfall, and *The Wedding*, both painted in 1787, and *Las
Gigantillas* and *Los Zancos* belonging to the following years. Final-
ly, in 1791, came *The Nincompoop* and *Blind Man's Buff*. Though
many people are of the opinion that Goya's greatest work is not to

be found among these designs for tapestry, it is unquestionable that they are more typical of him than any others, with their graceful portrayal of the clothes and customs of the people, and the rich colouring of which the artist was always master. Although Goya enjoyed making these designs they were the source of many complaints from the tapestry workers, who claimed that the number of figures, and their vari-coloured clothes, presented immense technical difficulties for the weavers, and that the artist's paintings were too detailed, and his models too complex, to lend themselves readily to reproduction.

Cruzada Villaamil wrote of them, «Goya must have had both pleasant and unpleasant memories of his work for the Tapestry Works. The pleasant aspect lay in the fact that these designs were responsible for drawing the attention of the Court to his work, and so led directly to his successful career as official Court Painter; the unpleasant associations being provoked by the spectacle of his original models being indifferently reproduced in another medium, many people judging his capacity by the reproductions rather than from the original paintings».

It is a fact that they were considered so unimportant for many years after Goya's death that they laid almost forgotten in one of the cellars of the Royal Palace until 1869 when, after careful restoration, they appeared in the Prado catalogue of the year 1876.

After the Goya designs the only remaining paintings to be seen on the Ground Floor are those in Halls LXXVI and LXXVII. These contain the most modern works on exhibition in the Prado, being composed of canvases by French and Spanish artists belonging to the period after Goya's death in 1828.

In order to visit these two halls it is best to return to the door by which we first entered the Ground Floor. Just opposite the small hall exhibiting the XIIth. century Maderuelo fresco, the entrance to Hall LXXVI is easily distinguished.

HALL LXXVI

The contents of this hall were presented to the Prado under the Will of Don Ramón de Errazu in 1904. They consist of nine pictures by Raimundo de Madrazo, nine by Mariano Fortuny—six oils and three water-colours—; five by the landscape painter Martín Rico, and one each by the French artists Meissonier and Paul Baudry.

We have always held the opinion that the Prado should exhibit nothing of a later date than the works of Goya, believing that the correct place for all such works is in one of Madrid's Modern Art Galleries, the Museo Romántico or the Museo Nacional de Arte Moderno.

In France they have established the principle, to which they strictly adhere that, 25 years after his death, an artist's works must be removed from the Luxembourg Gallery of modern art to the Louvre. Some people are in favour of a similar system in Spain, though we personally consider the period of 25 years far too short.

An objection to the Errazu Legacy, which is perhaps even more serious than that of not belonging to the historic tradition of the vast majority of the Prado's exhibits, is the fact that the pictures of which it is composed are frankly mediocre. An Art Gallery of the category of the Prado gains nothing by exhibiting the *Portrait of Queen María Cristina of Hapsburg* by Raimundo de Madrazo, or that of the Marchioness of Manzanedo by Meissonier, nor yet from the copy of Velázquez's head by Menipo; the small landscapes by Martín Rico; several of Fortuny's water-colours, and many others.

The best among the 25 pictures making up the Errazu Legacy are, in our view, the small nude study by Fortuny entitled *Women on the Sea Shore*, and Raimundo de Madrazo's portrait of the model Aline Masson wearing a white mantilla. The female nude by Madrazo, which is called *After the Bath*, strikes us as being inferior to *The Wave* by Baudry.

HALL LXXVII

Federico de Madrazo specialized in half-length portraits of Madrid's Society beauties of the mid-XIXth. century.

His portrait of the Countess of Vilches, painted in 1853, was a legacy to the Prado from the second Count of Vilches. Although somewhat overloaded and pompous, after the manner of Vicente

López, Madrazo still possesses a finer and more restrained touch than the Valencian artist.

The portraits of the Girona couple, dated 1856, were bequeathed by the Count of Eleta. Here it may be observed that Madrazo, although lacking the expressive simplicity of the great masters, portrays his figures with a certain ease of style, which reveals the effectiveness of his artistic training. These portraits came to the Prado in 1941, and that of the Countess of Vilches, three years later.

Don José de Madrazo's portrait of the Count of Vilches is notably inferior, as the father never achieved the capacity for portraiture possessed by his son, Federico. It was a legacy from the Count de la Cimera in 1944. The portrait of the Marchioness of Manzanedo, painted by Raimundo de Madrazo in Paris in 1875, is clearly superior to that of the same model made by Meissonier, though there is a certain lack of harmony in his employment of colour.

SECOND FLOOR

SOUTH WING

In addition to five lifts there are three large staircases by which the visitor may reach the First Floor. These are situated on the northern and southern side of the building and also in the centre. Two of these stairways continue from the Ist to the IInd. Floor. The IInd. Floor is divided into two separate groups of halls, one of which forms a north square and the other a south square, both possessing direct light. The two groups have no communication between them, and the visitor is obliged, therefore, after completing his tour of one group, to descend to the Ist. Floor, and then ascend again by the stairs leading to the other group.

The southern group of the IInd. Floor consists of eight halls: five devoted to Italian painting of the XVIIth. century; one to miscellaneous painting of the XVIIIth. century: one to the works of Anthony Mengs, and a small one to Lucca Giordano.

The northern group contains the Prado's Library, which is not open to the public, and nine exhibition halls. Five of these are devoted to the legacy of Fernández Durán; three to Spanish painting of the XVIIth. century, and one to drawings by Goya.

We have selected first to visit the southern group and, ascending the stairs marked LXXIX, upon which there are some Italian and Flemish canvases, we first enter the red silk tapestried hall LXXX, which is devoted to Mengs.

HALL LXXX

Anthony Raphael Mengs, born in Aussig in Bohemia, holds a rather special position in XVIIIth. century Spanish art. He lived in Spain for almost 10 years, and exercised a powerful influence upon his contemporaries, even when they were, like Goya, his artistic superiors. Mengs was not a great artist, prefering to concentrate all his efforts upon the elaboration of the conventional artistic theories of the time, which favoured the coldly studious rather than the inspirational, but he enjoyed enormous prestige during his lifetime. Mengs' admirers, such as José Nicolás de Azara, believed that he was destined to become a second Raphael, and his writings reveal that at one time he exercised something like an artistic dictatorship in Spain.

If we could not ourselves examine Mengs' work we should be obliged to accept the opinion of him expressed by his contemporaries, but the Prado contains no less than 22 of his canvases and, after viewing them, we are forced to the conclusion that these opinions greatly exaggerated his talent. Mengs' painting is cold and, as one critic puts it, «somehow a little tired», and his canvases always appear artificial and overburdened, and lacking in the essential grace and simplicity of line that is to be found in the work of all really great artists. The faces in his portraits often look as though they were made of porcelain, and all have an unattractively varnished appearance. Similarly, his works on religious themes fail to provoke any kind of enthusiasm, even the most important of them—his *Adoration of the Shepherds*, painted in Rome in 1770—lacking any kind of sincerity.

Mengs' portraits reveal some ability, their faulty technique being at least partly offset by accurate drawing and a clever use of colour when depicting his model's clothing. On the occasions when he managed to refrain from extensive, last minute, retouching, he could produce harmonious portraits, such as the head and shoulders of Maria Luisa of Parma. This is numbered 2568, and was bequeathed to the Prado by the Duke of Tarifa in 1934. Other good examples of Mengs' work are his portraits of King Charles IIIrd. and of Leopold, Grand Duke of Tuscany. His use of colour is well displayed in another of Maria Luisa of Parma, numbered 2189, and also in those of Maria Josefa de Lorraine, Archduchess of Austria; María Carolina of Lorraine, Queen of Naples, and of María Luisa de Bourbon, Grand Duchess of Tuscany. In all these portraits the painting of the dresses is exquisitely done.

Two other outstanding canvases by Mengs are his self-portrait, and that of the Prince who was later to become King Charles IVth.

In this same hall, which is mainly devoted to Mengs, there is a portrait of Anna von Muralt by the woman painter Angelica Kauffmann (1741-1807). Again the artist's reputation seems far in excess of her merits, and this canvas provides a fair example of the rigid German painting of the late XVIIIth. century. There is an attractive small portrait by the Italian artist Battoni, entitled *A Traveller in Italy* which, although no masterpiece, is pleasing.

> We leave Mengs' hall by the passage numbered LXXXI, which opens into three halls on each side. Those on the left hand are numbered LXXXII, LXXXIII and LXXXIV in the plan of the building. Before entering the second of these there is a small unnumbered hall containing 27 paintings by Lucca Giordano. The halls on the right of the passage are LXXXV, LXXXVI and LXXXVII, though, at the moment of writing, the doors are not marked in the usual way.

HALL LXXXV

This hall is devoted almost entirely to the work of Bassano, though it includes *Angels appearing to St. Jerome* by Il Dome-nichino; *St. Francis of Assisi,* by Agostino Carracci; *Portrait of a Venetian Noble,* by Tintoretto; *Portrait of a Venetian Girl,* by Tintoretta, and Titian's *Adoration of the Magi.*

The Bassanos were an artistic dynasty belonging to the Venetian School. There is nothing in the Prado by Francesco da Ponte, founder of the dynasty, though there are examples of the work of his more brilliant son Jacopo (1510?-1592) and of his grandsons Francesco and Leandro.

The signed *Last Supper,* by Francesco Bassano, was once in the possession of Elizabeth Farnesio. Notable among the works of Leandro are *The Miser and Lazarus* and *The Return of the Prodigal Son,* both of them being gifts to King Philip IVth. from the Duke of Medina de las Torres, though his three best canvases, in our opinion, are *Christ Expelling the Money-changers from the Temple*—numbered 27—, *Spring,* and the so far uncatalogued

Noah after the Deluge. In the next hall there are, additionally, Jacopo Bassano's *The Punishment of Adam*, a gift from Prince Philibert of Savoy to King Philip IVth., and *The Animals entering Noah's Ark*, bought by Titian for the Emperor Charles Vth. Jacopo Bassano is today considered as one of the founders of modern landscape painting, and was unquestionably the best painter of animals produced by the Renaissance. *The Punishment of Adam* and *The Animals entering Noah's Ark* both reveal a rich vitality, though all Bassano's works strike the modern critic as being too dark. It is unfortunate that the Prado does not contain any examples of Greco's work while he was in Italy as, if it did, we believe that it would be possible to prove that the same influences were present there as are to be perceived in Jacopo Bassano's style.

It is believed that Greco was a pupil of Jacopo for a time, and some of Bassano's works reveal the same vigour and spirituality which were so marked a characteristic of the Cretan's early style.

Bassano was an indifferent draughtsman, preferring to achieve his effects by contrasting light and shade, but he is a typical master of the Venetian School of painting.

HALL LXXXVI

Apart from the two canvases by Jacopo Bassano already mentioned this hall contains a number of original works of great interest, together with others which clearly reveal the decadence which overtook Italian art during the XVIth. century. The painters represented in this hall are the following: Titian, Tintoretto, Domenichino, Parmigianino, Sassoferrato, Guido Reni, Andrea Vaccaro, Bernardo Strozzi, Lionello Spada, Annibale Carracci, Guercino, Orazio Gentileschi, Camilo Procaccini, Federico Barocci and Tintoretto's daughter. Additionally, there are a number of works attributed to Jacopo del Conte and Antonio Barbalonga.

Two canvases by Sassoferrato are outstanding, *The Virgin and Child*, and *The Virgin of Meditation*. Both are carefully executed against a background of clear grey, and the sleeping Child in the former is really charming. They were bought by King Charles IVth. *The Assumption*, by the younger of the Carraccis, is a fine piece of altar painting, and was brought from Italy by the Count of Monterrey during the reign of King Philip IVth.

Procaccini has here two versions on the theme *Virgin with the Infant Jesus,* of which the uncatalogued one numbered 293 seems to us the better. *The Nativity* by Barocci—another purchase by King Charles IVth—reveals considerable originality in its composition.

The Veronica by Strozzi is so beautifully painted that, when it formed part if Elizabeth Farnesio's collection, it was ascribed to Velázquez.

We shall later see better examples of the works of Guido Reni and Guercino than are exhibited here. Titian's *Gethsemane* and the *Ecce Homo* ascribed to him are both dark and uninspiring.

The dominant personality in this hall is that of Tintoretto, as revealed by two powerful mythological canvases and a number of portraits by him. Among the portraits is one believed to be of Sebastiano Veniero, who was the leader of the Venetian fleet at the great Battle of Lepanto which, in our opinion, is the finest of all the 12 portraits by Jacopo Robusti Tintoretto possessed by the Prado. It was presented to King Philip IVth by the Marquess of Leganés.

The Wrath of Tarquin and *Judith & Holofernes,* though by no means Tintoretto's best work, are of great interest to the student of art, as they clearly reveal those special characteristics which brought the master fame, his handling of such a daring theme as the violation of Lucretia being typically vigorous.

Unfortunately, the quality of the work is not uniform, and our own preference is for *Judith & Holofernes,* which we believe to be one ot the finest from the brush of Tintoretto, the extraordinary brilliance with which he has captured the flesh tones being almost unequalled. It was bought by King Charles IIIrd from the collection of the Marquess de la Ensenada.

The Death of St. Cajetan by Vaccaro; *Abraham's Sacrifice* by Domenichino; and *St. Agatha in Prision,* ascribed to Barbalonga, are all unremarkable—*Abraham's Sacrifice* especially revealing both faulty composition and brush work.

HALL LXXXVII

Over 20 paintings are on exhibition here, but all are of inferior quality to those already seen in Hall LXXXVI.

Among the artists of whose work we have already seen examples there is a portrait by Tintoretto; a *Virgin and Child*, by Andrea del Sarto, which is not catalogued, and a *Holy Family* by Parmigianino. New to us, on this visit to the Prado, are Girolamo da Carpi, with a portrait believed to be of Alfonso IInd. of Este; Danielli da Volterra's, *The Annunciation;* Padovanino's, *Orpheus;* Michele Parrasio's, *Allegory,* and also his *Christ Adored by Pope St. Pius Vth;* the self-portrait of Artemisia Gentileschi; Salviati's, *Virgin and Child with two Angels;* the *Noli me Tangere* by Giulio Romano and Gianfrancisco Penni; Antonio Campi's *St. Jerome; The Holy Family* by Domenico Puligo; another on the same subject by Lucca Cangiaso; and *Charity* by Carlo Portelli. Additionally, the figures of St. Jerome, St. Margaret and St. Francis, portrayed on a single canvas by Giacomo and Giulio Francia; the *Portrait of a Physician*, by Lucia Anguisciola; a *Noli me Tangere* by Perino del Vaga, and works by various other Italian artists. In our opinion, the best among all these are two portraits, by Tintoretto and Carpi; the *Allegory*, by Parrasio, and the works of Volterra and Padovanino.

CORRIDOR (LXXXI)

Here again we are before the work of a number of Italian artists, from which we select the following: *The Battle* and *The Gladiators*, by Angelo Falcone; *St. John the Baptist*, by Francesco Solimena; *Noah after the Flood*, by Castiglione; *The Crucifixion*, by Giovanni Domenico Tiepolo; *View of Venice*, by Van Vitelli, and *The Fighting Women* and *David's defeat of Goliath* ascribed, respectively, to Vaccaro and Caravaggio. Additionally, there is a really beautiful *Descent from the Cross* believed to be a copy of the original by Volterra, and some landscapes by Gasparo Dughet.

NOTE. Before entering Hall LXXXIII we propose taking a brief glance at the numerous canvases by Lucca Giordano (1632-1705).

This vehement Neapolitan was, like Tiepolo, far more successful as a painter of frescos than of pictures. Both required the freedom of large wall or ceiling surfaces to achieve their effects and, confined to the limits of a canvas, the results give us no real idea of their capacity, and the work before us reveals the superficiality of an artist unsuccessfully attempting to adapt himself to a medium that is not his own. Most of Giordano's oil-paintings lack either accurate drawing or attractive colouring, and some are the merest sketches. One of these sketches is particularly effective, however, showing that the artist was better at conveying figures in movement than when stationary: this is entitled *The Defeat of Sisara.*

It is related that when he was very young Giordano's father, anxious for present profits rather than future fame, used continually to be shouting, *Luca, fa presto—Hurry up, Lucca*—and the phrase has stuck to him, even to this day, as a nickname and also a commentary upon his style and methods.

Lucca Giordano spent 10 years at the Royal Court of Spain, being summoned there by King Charles IInd in May 1692. He worked far too rapidly for it to be possible for him to give his paintings their proper finish, though this is less apparent in his decorative work which, seen from a distance, is ornamentally effective. However, when reduced to the limits of oil-paintings, such as are on view here, he betrays himself as an unworthy successor to Velázquez and Murillo.

NOTE. Hall LXXXII is at present closed.

HALL LXXXIII

There are 18 large canvases by XVIIth. century Italian painters on exhibition here, and examination of them serves to emphasize once again just what an extraordinary phenomenon was their contemporary Velázquez, working, for all his formative years, far away from what was then the acknowledged centre of the artistic world.

The artists whose work is now before us are Guido Reni, Guercino, Vaccaro, Danielli Crespi, Andrea Sacchi, Orazio and Artemisia Gentileschi, Pietro Novelli, and the Knight Massimo Stanzione, all of whom closely followed the precepts of Italian art as laid down during the previous century. They were heirs to the tremendous artistic achievements of their immediate predecessors, whose ideas they sought faithfully to follow. The result in itself is admirable but, in failing to allow for any kind of change or development to take its natural course, they bequeathed nothing to their own successors, and so initiated the period of complete decadence in Italian painting that was to follow.

The five outstanding canvases in this hall are, in our opinion, *The Seated Virgin*, and *St. Sebastian* both by Reni; *Piety*, by Crespi, and his *Susanna and the Elders*, which is particularly fine, revealing both mastery of design and accurate drawing of the human figure. Yet, despite their great merits, there is something lacking here which is unmistakably present in the works of Velázquez and Titian. It is only after careful analysis that we perceive their total absence of originality in thought, conception, feeling or execution.

Guido Reni and Guercino were notable masters of the eclectic Bolognese School of painting. Reinach, a prominent art historian, wrote, «The sad phenomenon of the decay of Italian Art has been attributed to many different causes. Some assert that it was a consequence of Italy's loss of independence, first under Spanish and then under Austrian domination. Others believe that the Counter-Reformation was responsible. However, whatever the true explanation may be, there is no denying the fact that XVIIth. century Italian art is forced, and the sentimental ecstasies and physical tortures of its martyrs profoundly unconvincing. The half-length paintings of it's *Virgins* and *Christs* show us an admiration for a new and sickly kind of piety—eyes always lugubriously raised to Heaven—which would not have been tolerated a century earlier. Titian's and Giorgione's Venus, and Raphael's Graces and Galateas, have now been replaced by the demonstratively penitent Magdalene

—whom Morelli described as «a Venetian Venus painted in the Jesuitical manner»—whose figure and expression reveal a slightly nauseating blend of sensuality and devotion.

«It is remarkable that what we might call the Jesuitical manner, which had so fatal an effect upon Italian art, yet produced masterpieces in the Flemish School of Rubens and his disciples. Perhaps the explanation lies in the natural, but stultifying, reverence with which the Italian artists of the XVIth. century regarded the great Masters of the Renaissance, which led them to neglect the essential study of Nature in favour of achieving a certain kind of almost mechanical perfection.»

We feel that this explanation very ably analyses the principal reasons why Italian art entered into a period of unmistakable decline at just the moment when Spain and the Low Countries were enjoying their Golden Age.

Guido Reni's *Seated Virgin*, which is a good example of the Bolognese School, was the property of King Philip IVth, and was one of the many art treasures looted by the retreating army of Joseph Bonaparte, but which were returned after Waterloo. Reni's canvas entered the Prado in 1837.

The fine *St. Sebastian*, by the same artist, formed part of Elizabeth Farnesio's collection, as did also the notable *St. Augustine Meditating on the Trinity*, painted by Guercino in 1636.

Guercino's *Susanna and the Elders*, painted almost 20 years before *St. Augustine*, was completed when the artist was still in his twenties, and is generally considered his best work. It reveals the influence of Caravaggio, and formerly hung in the Royal Appartments of the Escorial Palace. The wonderfully modelled nude figure of Christ, signed by Crespi and entitled *Piety*, was bought for the Royal collection at the time of the public auction of the Marquess del Carpio.

All the five works by Massimo Stanzione possessed by the Prado are on exhibition here. These are the signed *Offering to Bacchus*, and four others which together comprise a series devoted to the life of St. John Baptist—his birth, his farewell to his parents, his preaching in the desert, and his death. All five have been in the Royal collection since the XVIIth. century, and fully reveal the impressive style of the *Knight Massimo*.

There are here two other representations of *The Birth of St. John the Baptist,* one by Sacchi and the other, which is signed, by Artemisia Gentileschi. Of the latter Longhi wrote, «it is the best Italian «interior» of the XVIIth. century».

HALL LXXXIV

The all too small group of British paintings possessed by the Prado comprises the outstanding exhibit of this hall. It includes portraits by Reynolds, Romney and Hoppner, the three outstanding exponents of British XVIIIth. century painting. There are also two Andalusian landscapes in oils by the eminent XIXth. century water-colourist David Roberts, who visited Spain during the «romantic» period in art. These are all that the Prado has by which to judge British art, and it is obviously inadequate.

The landscapes by Roberts, and the Reynolds portrait—the latter bought by the Ministry of Education—entered the Prado in 1943. The Romney portrait was a gift from the Duke of Arcos in 1935, while the Hoppner formed part of the Luis Errazu legacy of 1925.

The pick of this little collection of British artist is the oil-painting by Reynolds, though Romney's work is also very fine.

There are two portraits by the Swedish painter Wertmüller in this hall. That of an unknown lady strongly recalls the style of Goya, the Aragonese painter, incidentally, being Wertmüller's senior by 5 years.

Other XVIIIth. century artists to be seen here are the Italians Antonio Joli, Giovanni Domenico Tiepolo and Canaletto, and the Spanish painters Luis Paret, Francisco and Ramon Bayeu. Joli is represented by two versions of *Charles IIIrd. Embarking in Naples;* Paret with the large canvas, *The Royal Couples,* which is inferior to his other works, and the Bayeu brothers by various oil-paintings of no particular merit. Also to be seen here are four of Tiepolo's eight scenes of *The Passion of Christ,* painted for the Madrid Church of St. Philip Neri. Three more of this series are on exhibition on the first floor of the Prado, and the eighth in the Corridor numbered LXXXI.

Although the Catalogue ascribes the *Views of Venice* to Giovanni Antonio Canal, known as Canaletto, it is by no means sure that the claim is justified. They form part of a legacy made to the Prado by Don Xavier Laffite in 1930, and certainly maintain the reputation for delicate colouring for which Canaletto is renowned.

NORTHERN WING OF THE SECOND FLOOR

On the stairway connecting the Ist. Floor with the northern wing of the IInd. Floor the following works by Spanish and Italian painters are to be seen; *Auto de Fe,* by Francisco Rizi; *The Vocation of St. Matthew,* by Juan de Pareja; *Render unto Caesar,* by Antonio Arias; *The Hunting Party,* by Mazo, and the canvases known as *A King of Spain* and *Two Kings of Spain,* both ascribed to Alonso Cano.

Rizi's large panel, crowded with figures, has more historical than artistic value. It is signed and dated 1683, and records different aspects of the sentences carried out by the Inquisition in the Plaza Mayor of Madrid, in the presence of King Charles IInd, on June 30th, 1680.

Don Pedro de Madrazo, author of *Detailed Catalogue of the Prado,* devotes considerable attention to this picture. However, it is so dark as to be difficult to examine effectively.

There are very few examples of the work of Pareja, the almost slavish disciple of Velázquez. His large *Vocation of St. Matthew,* signed and dated 1661, while still revealing the Master's influence, does so to a less marked extent than is usual in Pareja's pictures.

Velázquez's inspiration is more obvious in Mazo's *Hunting Party in Aranjuez,* where the artist's special talent for landscape provides the background for various groups of figures.

It is a picture, dexterously painted in varying tones of grey, which gives us an interesting glimpse of the fashions and customs of the period. It was bought by the Prado in 1934 from a Munich collector, with funds left by the Count of Cartagena. It formed part of the Royal Collection in 1666, and was temporarily looted by Napoleon's elder brother Joseph.

The two canvases attributed to Alonso Cano, depicting three early Kings of Spain, were painted at some date during the first half of the XVIIth. century—probably between 1625 and 1645—as decoration for the old Royal Palace in Madrid. There are better examples of Cano's work to be seen in the Prado than is supplied by these three seated figures, but it must be borne in mind that they were painted with the foreshortened perspective required by their intended position on a high cornice in one of the Royal appartments, and that they were not designed by the artist to be seen, as is now the case, at close quarters.

HALL LXXXIX

Here there are a number of pictures by artists with whose work we are already familiar, such as Ribera, Ribalta, Carreño, Cano and Francisco Rizi. Additionally, there are canvases by Antonio del Castillo, Juan Antonio Escalante, Miguel Jacinto Meléndez, Jiménez Donoso and Luis Tristán, whose works we have not seen previously.

There are four paintings by the Castillian artist Luis Tristan in the possession of the Prado, two of which are not at present on exhibition, and the other two—both of them head and shoulder representations of Saints—are before us now. In the opinion of Palomino, Tristan's work closely resembled that of Velázquez. The two examples here were both part of a retable from the Church of Yepes—a village near Toledo—and both are signed and dated 1616. They came to the Prado in 1942.

In the opinion of some experts Tristan was the real founder of the Toledo School, of which Cruzada Villaamil wrote, «it is remarkable for its pleasant and delicate use of colour which, in its purity of tone, frequently recalls the work of Titian».

It is believed that Tristan may have studied under Greco but, although some of his works were attributed to the Cretan Master, the resemblance between the two is superficial.

According to Burger, Tristan was undoubtedly influenced by Greco and, unlike so many of his contemporaries, was able to

10

benefit by the teachings of the Venetian School without falling into the grave errors at that time being taught in Rome and Bologna.

The two heads by Tristan exhibited here are listed in the Prado catalogue as *St. Monica* and *The Weeping Saint*. Both are in a perfect state of preservation, and constitute an excellent example of Spanish painting of the late XVIth. century.

The two sketches by Meléndez are entitled, *St. Augustin Exorcising the Plague of Locusts*, and *The Burial of the Count of Orgaz* the latter, of course, being a subject immortalized by El Greco. Both these interesting sketches were made in 1725 for the Madrid Augustinian Monastery of St. Philip the Royal. They were transferred to the Museo de la Trinidad before reaching the Prado. For a time they were attributed to Sebastian Muñoz, though the present catalogue has corrected this error. Sánchez Cantón rates both of these pictures very highly, writing «they convey the very essence of the Madrilenian School during the reign of King Philip Vth. Both are beautifully finished works, in which the teachings of El Greco have been worthily upheld».

From the series of six canvases, illustrating the Old Testament story of Joseph by the Cordoban painter Antonio del Castillo, two only are on view. These are entitled, *Joseph Sold into Captivity* and *The Chastity of Joseph*.

They were intended for the Museo de la Trinidad, but came to the Prado in 1863, when they were purchased for 9.500 pesetas.

Neither is of outstanding merit, Castillo's style, in the opinion of Madrazo, being comparable to that of Caravaggio, and «distinguished by its harsh blending of colour».

Neither of the two pictures by Escalante, entitled *The Dead Christ* and *The Infant Jesus with St. John*, are of great interest, nor is the *St. Francis' Vision of Paula* by Donoso in any way remarkable. Writing of Donoso a critic many years ago observed that this follower of Herrera (el Mozo) appeared always to be looking for short cuts to enable him to achieve effects impossible without deep thought and preparation but that, despite this defect, his figures reveal a certain genuine ability.

The painter with the largest number of works on exhibition in this hall is Juan Carreño (1614-1685). These consist of two on religious themes—*St. Anne Instructing the Virgin* and *St. Sebastian*—and four full-length portraits, of Peter Ivanovitch Potemkin, Catherine the Great of Russia's Ambassador to Spain; of Francisco Bazán, a Court Jester; and two of the deformed child Eugenia Martínez Vallejo, one of them a nude study.

The four portraits were already in the Royal collection at the end of the XVIIth. century. King Ferdinand VIIth. presented the nude to the painter Juan Gálvez and, after passing through various hands, it reached the Prado in 1939 from Baron de Forna. The clothed study of the same unattractive subject came to the Prado in 1828, when it was attributed to Velázquez, though with the rider «ascribed by some people to Carreño».

Don Juan Carreño de Miranda was of a noble Asturian family, and is considered one of the most eminent of Spanish portraitists, even being compared to Velázquez though, in our opinion, without justification. The Prado contains seven portraits by Carreño, those of King Charles IInd. and his mother Queen Mariana, being in the Central Gallery, while that of the Duke of Pastrana is in the hall principally devoted to Velázquez, of which we have already had something to say.

This is enough to enable us to judge of his quality, and to appreciate his sense of realism and technical excellence in the Velázquez tradition. Cean Bermúdez wrote that Carreño was «the finest naturalist painter in the Castile of his day», though, in our opinion, Cossío was nearer the truth when he described him as «the greatest of all the Madrid School, with the sole exception of Velázquez».

While the nude study of the deformed child cannot be made attractive, Carreño manages to prevent it from being repulsive, and the modelling of the body is beautifully executed.

Examples of the work of Ribera are to be seen here, as well as later in Halls XC and XCI. Before us now is one of his more colourful canvases, *Isaac and Jacob*, which is signed and dated

1637. It was valued at 24.000 «reales» in 1794, and came to the Prado from the Academia de San Fernando in 1827. Its extraordinarily rich and beautiful tones of red and blue are strongly reminiscent of the great Venetian Masters.

St. Matthew and St. John, is by Ribera's master, Francisco Ribalta, and has been in the possession of the Prado since the publication of its first catalogue. Commenting upon this picture, Ribalta's biographer, Espresati remarks, «the figures are depicted with a vigorous realism, and it will be observed that the hands and feet of both saints have been painted with the most minute care. The clothes are suggested, in the manner typical of Ribera towards the end of his life, by sweeping folds and heavy masses of colour».

There is a *Virgin and Child* to be seen here by Alonso Cano, upon whose work we propose to comment when writing of Hall XCI.

HALL XC

This hall is dominated by Murillo and Ribera, whose styles have often been described, respectively, as «soft» and «rough», though the superficiality of this analysis becomes obvious as soon as we examine the examples of both artists to be seen here. Immediately a certain similarity between the supposed opposite extremes begins to emerge, particularly when we observe the essentially Spanish quality of both, even though Ribera was working in Naples and Murillo in Seville.

There are 16 canvases by Murillo on our right as we enter, and also *Benedict's Supper* by Friar Juan Rizi, and Valdés Leal's *Christ Disputing in the Temple.* On the left there are 27 pictures by Ribera, and also *Ezekiel's Vision* by Collantes, and Claudio Coello's portrait of Father Cabanillas.

Both Murillo and Ribera were intensely realistic in their style, a fact which is clearly revealed in their religious painting, where their figures of saints are untouched by the conventional idealization to be found in all the non-Spanish artists of the XVIth. and XVIIth. centuries.

This hall contains the following works by Murillo; *The Holy*

Family «del Pajarito», The Adoration of the Shepherds, The An-
nunciation, St. Anne and the Child Virgin, a half-length *Annun-*
ciation, The Vision of St. Francis, Rebecca and Elisha, St. Augustin
between Christ and the Virgin, The Martyrdom of St. Andrew,
and various other smaller pictures.

In the presence of this further collection of Murillo and Ribera
—with whose paintings we are already familiar from the First
Floor—the vigorous and earthy quality of the latter, and the
mellow finish so typical of the former, become still further apparent.

Perhaps the most famous of Murillo's works on exhibition
here is his *Holy Family,* showing the Virgin Mary, St. Joseph and
the Infant Jesus. The Infant is shown playing with a small white
dog, and the whole composition is of rare tenderness and charm.
It was painted in 1650 and, nearly a century later, was mentioned
in the catalogue of the Palace of La Granja as forming part of
Elizabeth Farnesio's collection. Napoleon's brother Joseph carried
it off to France, from whence it was returned in 1818. In 1794 it
was valued at 12.000 «reales».

Another of Murillo's canvases looted during the French invasion was *The Adoration of the Shepherds.* This was painted at
the same period as Velázquez's *Maids of Honour* and *The Spin-*
ners, and was valued at 30.000 «reales» in 1794. It provides an
excellent example of the realistic treatment of religious themes
that was so marked a characteristic of Spanish XVIIth. century
art. This is also true of the tranquil «interior» portraying St. Anne
teaching her little daughter the Virgin Mary, a picture which was
valued at 6.000 «reales» in 1794, and which also once formed
part of the Elizabeth Farnesio collection.

The Vision of St. Francis and *St. Augustin between Christ*
and the Virgin Mary form a pair for an altar-piece.

The former was bought by King Charles IVth, and the latter
by the Marquess de los Llanos.

With the *Murillos* to be seen here, together with those already visited on the First Floor, it is possible to form a clear impression of the artist's work as a whole. His style is gentle and
uncomplex and, in its intimate simplicity, is perhaps better suited
to the home than to the decoration of Church or Palace. He was
far more attracted to the portrayal of gentle Virgins and smiling

Infant Christs than he was to the dramatic and terrible scenes of
Christ's Passion and Death.

Despite changing fashions in Art, Murillo will never lack for
admirers. Gerardo Diego recognized that the Spanish people—and
women especially—have never waveved in their loyalty to Murillo, whatever may be the fluctuations of his prestige in other
countries. This loyalty outweighs the carping of critics, who are
often more concerned with being in the fashion of the moment
than they are with the eternal verities of Art.

Ribera painted with a much more virile brush, specializing
in rough, bearded types, that would never have interested Murillo.

Nevertheless, Ribera's *Trinity* contains some charming figures
of young angels, which shows that he was not insensitive to conventional physical beauty, but was more interested in the portrayal
of character than his younger contemporary.

Special mention must be made of Ribera's oil-painting entitled, *The Duelling Women*, signed and dated 1636, which is said
to record an incident which had taken place in Naples 84 years
previously in the presence of the Marquess del Vasto. Two women,
whose names are not known, fought a duel to decide which of them
should take the man whom they both sought for her lover. History
records that blood was shed, but does not tell us whether either
of the duellists was killed by her rival.

The *Annunciation* to be seen here is inferior to Ribera's famous
one in Salamanca—known as *La Concepción de Monterrey*—and
is also not so fine as Murillo's rendering of the same theme. It
was bought for 12.000 «reales» by King Ferdinand VIIth. in 1833.

The subject of the Immaculate Conception was particularly
popular with baroque artists, and the best Spanish examples are
undoubtedly those by Murillo and Ribera.

The half-length *St. Sebastian* is notable for Ribera's brilliant
modelling of the saint's body. It belongs to the Master's last years,
and once hung in Velázquez's studio, later becoming the property
of Queen María Luisa's favourite Godoy. Ribera painted the
Martyrdom of St. Sebastian several times, and those on exhibition
in the Bilbao and Valencia Galleries are both superior to that possessed by the Prado.

It is believed that Ribera's *Fable of Bacchus* was one of his finest works, but it was destroyed in the great fire that burned down the old Royal Palace in 1734, and we have before us only two fragments that were somehow saved. They are of two ivy-crowned profiles—one a woman and the other of an old man—and reveal entirely new aspects of Ribera's art. They are catalogued 1122 and 1123.

Friar Juan Rizi's *St. Benedict's Supper* is a most powerful and moving portrayal of a scene illuminated by artificial light, in which the sober, yet intense colouring makes a strong appeal to the senses.

It was painted for the Monastery of St. Millan de la Cogolla, and reached the Prado from the Museo de la Trinidad.

Christ Disputing in the Temple by Valdés Leal was bought for 3.000 pesetas in 1880. Writing of it Beruete says, «It is typical of the intensity of Valdés' work towards the end of his life. Though not a masterpiece it marks an essential stage in the artist's development, and is one of the very few pictures in existence belonging to his last years.»

The Prado contains only a single example of the work of the Madrid painter Francisco Collantes, who was born in the same year as Velázquez. This is *The Resurrection of the Flesh* as seen by Ezekiel, signed and dated 1630, and belonging to the Royal collection since the time of King Philip IVth. It was one of the 50 pictures sent to France at the orders of Joseph Bonaparte, but was returned in 1816. After 11 years in the Academia de San Fernando it was presented to the Prado. Palomino refers to it as «a work of great imagination and ability», while a later critic wrote, «it is a brilliant exposition of the artist's capacity as designer, colourist and anatomist, as well as a man deeply versed in architectural composition».

HALL XCI

This hall contains works by Ribera, Alonso Cano, Murillo, Valdés Leal, Claudio Coello, Francisco Antolínez, Jusepe Leonardo and Juan de Sevilla. Two among the seven pictures by Murillo deserve special mention. The first is that numbered 1075 in the

Catalogue, and entitled *St. Paul the Hermit*, signed and dated 1640; and the second the portrait of the blind sculptor Giovanni Gambassi, also signed and dated 1632. Both bear the unmistakable characteristics of the artist who was described as «the leader of XVIIth. century Spanish painting».

Alonso Cano, sculptor and architect, influenced Spanish XVIth. century art in much the same way as Michael Angelo inspired that of Italy during the preceding century. The Prado contains nine pictures by him, the seven best of which are here. One other is exhibited on the Ground Floor, and the ninth is in store.

Among those before us now are the following four outstanding canvases; two versions of *Christ Supported by an Angel*, *The Virgin and Child*, and *St. Benedict's Vision*. *St. Benedict's Vision* is listed in the catalogue of the Alcázar Palace in Madrid for the year 1700, while the *Virgin and Child* was bought by King Charles IVth. Of the two versions of *Christ Supported by an Angel* one was bought from the Marquess de la Ensenada in 1769, and the other—the only signed one—came to the Prado under the Bosch legacy.

There is no recorded work by Alonso Cano which entitles him to be considered a really great artist, despite the rich colouring of his paintings in Granada Cathedral, and various of his canvases here in the Prado which are also deserving of admiration.

Cano began his apprenticeship in Seville at the same time as Velázquez and Zurbarán but, unlike his great contemporaries, Cano was less sure of the line he wished to pursue and, like Michael Angelo, was really more interested in sculpture than in painting. However, his pictures are nearly always of a very high quality, and some, such as his *St. Agnes* now in the Berlin Museum, have all the characteristics to be found in the best of Zurbarán's works. The silver and grey tones employed by Cano bring some of Velázquez's portraits to mind but, occasionally, his colouring is harsh and unclear. In short, Alonso Cano was a painter of uneven quality, though always displaying a sense of taste and beauty in the mature and classic style of the XVIIth. century.

There are four small oil-paintings by Murillo on exhibition here, which served as preliminary sketches for the finished canvases in the possession of the London collector Otto Beit, on the theme of the Prodigal Son. These sketches were in the Royal Palace in Madrid in 1814, and appear in the first Prado catalogue. It is believed that they were painted towards the end of Murillo's life.

Three sketches by the Seville painter Francisco Antolínez, are on exhibition here. They represent scenes from the Life of the Virgin Mary—*The Presentation, The Betrothal* and *The Nativity*— and form part of a series of six. Two others, *The Adoration of the Magi* and *The Flight into Egypt,* are kept in store, and the sixth, *The Annunciation,* is in Vigo.

It is believed that all were painted in Seville for the Convent of St. Philip el Real in Madrid, and reached the Prado from the Museo de la Trinidad. They are not of great merit, and Cruzada Villaamil wrote, «the painter was nicknamed by amateurs *Antolínez the Bad* in order to differentiate him from his uncle Don José. He disliked painting, although it was his sole source of livelihood, as his various visits to Madrid in search of other employment were always unsuccessful».

Claudio Coello's *The Infant Christ* was bought by the Prado in 1935 from a Madrid antiquary. For many years it was in France, where it was ascribed to Carlo Dolci. However, when it was cleaned Coello's signature was discovered, together with the date 1660, when the artist must have been only 18 years old.

There are very few works by the XVIIth. century Aragonese artist Jusepe Leonardo, whose career was cut short by insanity before he was 40. The Prado contains three of his canvases, two of them on historical themes which may be seen on the Ist. Floor, and the religious picture, now before us, entitled *The Birth of the Virgin Mary.* The first two were ordered by King Philip IVth. for the Salon de Reinos in the Retiro Palace, while the *Birth of the Virgin* was bought for the Museo de la Trinidad in 1864 for 10.000 «reales».

These three canvases are enough to convince us of the artist's real quality, after the Velázquez manner, and in the opinion of Señor Tormo, «if he had lived longer, and retained his faculties, he might well have become a worthy successor to Spain's greatest master».

The Presentation of the Virgin in the Temple by Valdés Leal, and the *Rich Man's Feast and Lazarus* by Juan de Sevilla are of no outstanding interest. Sevilla was an Andalusian disciple of Pedro de Moya, who sought to follow the style of Van Dyck. Sevilla himself was a great admirer of Rubens, and his paintings clearly reveal the fact.

The portrait of a child of about 12, by an unknown artist, which may be seen here is worthy of brief special mention. It is known that the child was the son of Francisco Ramos del Manzano, a lawyer who died towards the close of the XVIIth. century. It is a sober, clear painting, in which various shades of grey are predominant, and it reveals traces of the brush of Velázquez. It was bought for the Prado for 30.000 pesetas from the antiquary Borondo in 1930.

HALLS XCII, XCIII, XCIV, XCV AND XCVI

These five halls contain the pictures bequeathed to the Prado 20 years ago by Don Pedro Fernández Durán—«in memory of my father and mother, Don Miguel Fernández Durán and Doña Paula Bernaldo de Quirós, Marquesses of Perales and Tolosa»— to quote a plaque displayed here.

The legacy consisted of 80 pictures, mostly by non-Spanish artists, and a number of drawings, miniatures, arms, tapestries, sculptures, etc. The entire legacy is not on exhibition owing to lack of space, and only 50 out a collection of 3.000 drawings are to be seen here. These halls were inaugurated on June 18th, 1931, but the pictures were not hung until the conclusion of the 1942 catalogue. Among the pictures are works by Goya, Van der Weyden, Morales and Herrera (the Elder), and the largest individual representation is the twelve by the Flemish painter Franck (the Younger). Perhaps the most valuable part of the legacy consists of the five canvases by Goya, which are his *Portrait of General Ricardos, The Colossus, Blind Man's Buff, The Drunken Builder,* and *The Hermitage of St. Isidor.*

Other painters, whose work is represented in the Durán legacy, are the Spaniards, Orrente, Juan de Toledo, Carnicero and Ferro;

the Italians, Giordano, Maratti, Amiconi and Caracciolo; the Flemish, Coffermans, Neefs (the Elder), Joris van Son, Frans Ikens, Van Kessel (the Elder), Teniers and Brouwer; the Dutch, Heda, Pieter Claeszon and Wouvermann; the French, Pillement, Oudry and Boullogne, and the German Vollardt.

Some of these painters were not represented in the Prado until the Durán legacy was made.

HALL XCVII

This hall is the only one devoted exclusively to Francisco Goya. Here his whole dynamic personality is revealed to us in the quick markings of brush, pencil and pen, often scrawled on odd pieces of paper in order to catch some fleeting idea of Goya's extraordinary imagination. The impression is of a brain literally bursting with ideas and figures, which the hand turns in a moment to brilliant life.

Of these drawings 186 were bought in 1866 for the Museo de la Trinidad for 500 «escudos» by Don Ramón de la Huerta, from whence they came to the Prado. Over 250 more were bought in 1886 from Don Mariano Carderera, and a total of 472 are on exhibition today, most of them being preliminary sketches for the four famous engravings, known as *The Caprices, The Horrors of War, Los Disparates* and *La Tauromaquia.* The drawings bought by Don Ramón de la Huerta belong to the last phase of Goya's life, some of them having been made in Bordeaux, where he died in 1828.

Goya employed all manner of things in executing his drawings—black and red pencil, chalk, brush and pen—and also used water-colours made from Indian ink, sepia, red earth, ordinary ink, and many other unusual ingredients. Almost all these drawings were made without the employment of a model yet, with a few lines, Goya managed to capture the essential qualities of form and expression in his subjects. Many of the drawings here are political satires, or in censure of popular vices, yet he is always preaching the doctrines of liberty and tolerance, and the drawings reveal his extraordinary mastery of line, movement, depth and perspective.

Some years ago Don Félix Boix, in writing of these drawings said, «The development of Goya into one of the most extraordinary artists that the world has ever seen is here clearly revealed. His lack of culture was counterbalanced by his amazing capacity for observation, and the possession of an almost uncanny intuition, which enabled him accurately to imagine things he had never seen. At the same time he was a complete master of all the means by which he could achieve his supreme purpose—the exact reproduction of the character, movement, life and spirit of the world he saw around him. In this he stands alone.»

SCULPTURE

We have omitted reference of sculpture until now in order not to interfere with the main object of this book, which is a study of the paintings to be seen in the Prado.

However, as long ago as 1908, Don Eduardo Barrón catalogued no less than 400 examples of sculpture here and, since then, the number has been increased. But, although some of these are of real artistic value, they are frequently regarded as little more than an ornament to halls and galleries visited in order to see the pictures.

There are very few on the Second Floor, but there are some fine examples of sculpture in the Central Gallery, and the best are on the Ground Floor, where there are two halls devoted exclusively to them. The larger of these—Hall LVIII—contains no less than 800 statues, there being a special catalogue of its contents by Don Elías Tormo, entitled *The Hall of the Muses*.

In Hall LXXI there are twelve works exhibited in niches, including the famous pre-Christian *Lady of Elche*, and the three examples of Ancient Greek and Sumerio-Arcadian art bequeathed to the Prado in 1943 by the Mexican, Don Mario de Zayas.

The bust of an Iberian priestess, known as *The Lady of Elche* came to the Prado in 1941 from the Louvre in Paris, where it had been since the beginning of the century. It is an important example of Iberian sculpture produced about 500 B. C., and was discovered on August 4th., 1897, in Alcudia, near Elche, by the French Archaeologist Pierre Paris. It was sold by the owner of the land on which it was discovered to Pierre Paris who presented it to the Louvre. It is made of calcareous stone with a faint trace of colouring, which suggests that it may have been the work of a Greek artist.

Nearly all the sculpture contained in the Prado came from the Royal Collection, and may be divided into two groups: the Greco-Roman, and the work of the XVIth. to XIXth. centuries. There are no examples of mediaeval sculpture. As is inevitable in such a collection there are a number of pieces of unknown origin. Many pieces were part of the collections made by King Philip Vth. and his wife, Elizabeth Farnesio—this remarkable Queen bringing with her from Rome a quantity of statuary that had formerly been the property of Queen Christina of Sweden. There are additionally the pieces collected by the Emperor Charles Vth., and his son King Philip IInd. and also the gifts sent to Charles Vth. by Pope Paul IInd, and to Philip IInd. by Cardinal Montepulciano in 1561. Thirty Roman busts were presented to King Charles IVth, by the diplomat Don José Nicolás de Azara, who had purchased them in Italy. Lastly, there are a few pieces from the collection bought by Velázquez, when in Italy, at the orders of King Philip IVth.

Writing of the sculpture to be seen in the Prado, Camon says, «The greater part belongs to the Graeco-Roman period—a term which is admittedly inexact, but which cannot be avoided owing to the impossibility of separating the two overlapping civilizations. Many are, for example, Roman copies from Greek originals but, either directly or indirectly, Hellenic art is fairly represented here. The earliest examples are the representations of Apollo, which form part of the Zayas Legacy; then comes Aristogiton's head from the famous *Tyrannicides* group owned by the Naples Museum, which belongs to the early Vth, century B. C. The classic period of Greek sculpture is splendidly represented by a statue of the Diadumeno, inspired by that of Policleto.

There are more abundant traces of Phidias than of Praxiteles —his sensual and graceful style being immediately apparent—and there are a few examples of the passionate art of Scopa.

The series of busts are of the first importance, including the

Greek—or Roman copies of the Greek originals—of Homer, Plato and Aristotle. The purely Roman ones are of Augustus, Lucio Vero and Caracalla, besides two splendid representations of Antinoo.»

Among the classical marble statues there are some striking examples of Phidias' School, notably the head of an Athenian horse, and a male torso in hall LXXI, this latter forming part of the Zayas Legacy.

Belonging to the Hellenic period *The Venus of the Shell* and *Hipnos* are of special value, while the Praxiteles School claims the so-called *Group of St. Alphonsus* (perhaps representing Castor and Pollux) and also the *Faun and Kid, The Venus of the Dolphin* and *Aphrodite* bequeathed by Zayas.

Among the statues belonging to the late Renaissance period mention must be made of the Italians Leone and Pompeo Leoni, who left some admirable bronzes in Spain.

The Prado also contains the statue of the *Emperor Charles Vth.* in the Rotunda, and the armed figure of King Philip IInd. in Hall XXI.

THE DAUPHIN'S TREASURE

HALL LXXIII (GROUND FLOOR)

This famous treasure is composed of a number of fine jewelled chalices, inherited by King Philip Vth. of Spain from his father, the Dauphin. The Dauphin, as the eldest son, was heir presumptive to King Louis XIVth of France, but pre-deceased «le roi Soleil» by three years.

It would appear that Philip Vth. received this inheritance without much interest, and ordered the whole collection to be sent to the Palace at La Granja, where it remained for several years. In 1734 it was catalogued, revealing that it consisted of 86 gems, set in gold, enamel or cameo, of which 71 are on exhibition here. To this number must be added the 49 pieces worked in rock crystal. All 120 are the work of Italian or French artists of the XVIth. and XVIIth. centuries.

Matilde López Serrano wrote of the Dauphin's Treasure, «It is only by recalling something of the history of France that we can understand how such treasure came into the possession of the House of Bourbon. The strong personal rivalry between the Emperor Charles Vth. of Spain and King Francis Ist. of France led to constant wars on Italian soil for the possession of Milan and the Kingdom of Naples, where the French monarch fell in love with the art, culture and luxury of the Renaissance, and employed a number of Italian artists to beautify his Court.»

The Dauphin's Treasure was accumulated, therefore, by the last of the Valois and the early Bourbon Kings, a time when Italian craftsmanship was at its best. Formerly part of the Louvre collection it can only be compared with those to be seen in Vienna, Munich and Florence.

When, in 1776, King Charles IIIrd. of Spain founded the Royal Museum of Natural History he presented the entire collection to it but, during the period of the Napoleonic invasion, most of it was carried off to Paris, from whence it was returned after the Battle of Waterloo in 1815. However, by then 12 pieces had disappeared, and many among the remainder had been seriously damaged.

They have been on exhibition in the Prado since 1839, largely due to the efforts of Don José de Madrazo, who appreciated their artistic worth and, in 1886, they were repaired by the goldsmith Pedro Zaldos. During the Civil War, in 1937, the collection was again sent abroad, but returned in 1939.

The gems themselves are of diverse kinds; agate, turquoise, jasper, jade and lapizlazuli. Most of the agates are white, yellow, or a faint purple shade, while the jaspers are nearly all of a deep green colour, which contrasts attractively with the softer green of the jade, and the blue of the lapizlazuli and turquoises. Nearly all are set in enamelled gold or silver-gilt. Some of the finest examples of the gold and silver-smith's art are decorated by diamonds, emeralds, rubies, garnets, turquoises and blister pearls.

Eleven pieces of the Dauphin's Treasure were stolen from the Prado in 1918, the robbery being discovered in September. The missing objects were never recovered, and the incident led to the resignation of the then Director and Assistant Director of the Prado.

ALPHABETICAL INDEX

OF THE PRINCIPAL PAINTERS REPRESENTED IN THE PRADO,
WITH THE NUMBER OF THEIR WORKS, THE HALLS WHERE THEY
MAY BE SEEN, AND THE PAGE NUMBERS WHERE MENTION
OF THEM IS MADE

AMBERGER, CHRISTOF.—German. Born between 1500 and 1510; died about 1562.—Two portraits in HALL LIX. (Page 115.)

ANGELICO, FRA (GUIDO DI PIETRO DA MUGELLO).—Italian. Born in Vicchio di Mugello (Florence) in 1387; died in Rome in 1455.—One picture in HALL III. (Page 42.)

ANTOLINEZ, FRANCISCO.—Spanish. Born in Sevilla in 1644; died in Madrid in 1700.—Three pictures in HALL XCI. (Page 153.)

ANTOLINEZ, JOSÉ.—Spanish. Born in Madrid in 1635; died in Madrid in 1675.—Two pictures in HALL XXIX. (Page 101.)

ARELLANO, JUAN DE.—Spanish. Born in Santorcaz (Madrid) in 1614; died in Madrid in 1676.—Eight flower studies in HALL LXXII. (Page 122.)

ARGUIS, MASTER OF.—Spanish. Unknown Aragonese painter of the mid 15th. century.—Pieces from a retable in HALL L. (Page 115.)

BALDUNG, HANS.—German. Born in Weyersheim between 1476 and 1485; died in 1545.—Two pictures in HALL XLIV. (Page 35.)

BASSANO, JACOPO DA PONTE.—Italian. Born in Bassano between 1510 and 1515; died in 1592.—Seven pictures in HALLS VI, LXXXV and LXXXVI. (Pages 136 and 137.)

BAYEU, FRANCISCO.—Spanish. Born in Zaragoza in 1734; died in Madrid in 1795.—Six pictures in HALLS XXXI and XXXIV. (Page 109.)

BELLINI, GIOVANNI.—Italian. Born in Venice or Padova, about 1430; died in Venice in 1516.—One picture in HALL IV. (Page 43.)

BENSON, AMBROSIUS.—Flemish. Born in Bruges; died in 1550.—Seven pictures in HALL LIX. (Page 115.)

BERMEJO, BARTOLOMÉ.—Spanish. Born in Córdoba, and painted between 1474 and 1495.—One picture in HALL XXIV. (Page 38.)

BERRUGUETE, PEDRO.—Spanish. Believed to have been born in Paredes de Nava (Palencia) about 1450; died about 1503.—Fourteen pictures in HALLS XXIV, XLV and L. (Pages 37 and 38.)

BOEL, Peter.—Flemish. Born in Antwerp in 1622; died in Paris, in 1674.—Four pictures in HALLS LXI, LXII and XVII. (Page 117.)

BOSCH, Hieronymus Van Aeken.—Dutch. Born in Bois-le-Duc about 1450; died in 1516.—Six works in HALL XLIII, and one in HALL XLIV. (Pages 32 to 34.)

BOTTICELLI, Sandro (Alessandro Filipepi).—Italian. Born in Florence in 1444 or 1445; died there in 1510.—Three pictures in HALL III. (Pages 42 and 43.)

BOURDON, Sébastien.—French. Born in Montpellier in 1616; died in Paris in 1671.—Two pictures in HALL XLIX. (Page 126.)

BOUTS, Thierry or Dieric.—Flemish. Born in Harlem about 1420; died in Louvain in 1475.—One triptych in HALL XL. (Page 28.)

BRONZINO, Il (Agnolo di Cosimo Allori).—Italian. Born in Monticelli (near Florence) in 1503; died in Florence in 1572.—One portrait in HALL V. (Page 45.)

BRUEGHEL, the Old, Peeter.—Flemish. Born probably in Brueghel (Dutch Brabante) about 1525; died in Brussels in 1569.—One picture in HALL XLIII. (Page 31.)

BRUEGHEL DE VELOURS, Jan.—Flemish. Born in Brussels in 1568; died in Antwerp in 1625. Twenty seven pictures in HALLS XIX, XX, XXI, XXIII and LXIV. (Page 96.)

CABEZALERO, Juan Martín.—Spanish. Born in Almadén (Ciudad Real) in 1633; died in Madrid in 1673.—One picture in HALL XXIX. (Page 102.)

CALLET, Antoine François.—French. Born in Paris in 1741; died in Paris in 1825.—One portrait in HALL XLIX. (Page 126.)

CANALETTO, Il (Giovanni Antonio Canal).—Italian. Born in Venice in 1697; died there in 1768.—Three pictures in HALL LXXXIV. (Page 144.)

CANO, Alonso.—Spanish. Born in Granada in 1601; died there in 1667.—Eight pictures in HALLS LXXIV, LXXXVIII, LXXXIX and XCI. (Pages 122, 145 and 152.)

CARNICERO, Antonio.—Spanish. Born in Salamanca in 1748; died in Madrid in 1814.—Four pictures in HALLS XXXI and XCIV. (Page 110.)

CARRACCI, Annibale.—Italian. Born in Bologna in 1560; died in Rome in 1609.—Eight pictures in HALLS LXXXI, LXXXVI and LII. (Page 137.)

CARREÑO DE MIRANDA, Juan.—Spanish. Born in Avilés in 1614; died in Madrid in 1685.—Nine pictures in HALLS XIII, XXVII and LXXXIX. (Page 147.)

CASTILLO, Antonio del.—Spanish. Born in Córdoba in 1616 and died there in 1668.—Two pictures in HALL LXXXIX. (Page 146.)

CATENA, IL (VINCENZO DI BIAGIO).—Italian. Believed to have been born in Venice about 1470 and died there in 1531.—One picture in HALL IV. (Page 43.)

CEREZO, MATEO.—Spanish. Born in Burgos about 1626; died in Madrid in 1666. Three pictures in HALL XXIX. (Page 101.)

CLAESZON VAN REYMERSWAELE, MARINUS.—Dutch. Born in Zeeland towards the end of the 15th. century; died in 1567.—One picture in HALL XLIV, and another in HALL LX. (Page 116.)

COELLO, CLAUDIO.—Spanish. Born in 1642, in Madrid, where he died in 1693.—Seven pictures in HALLS XXIX, LXXIV, XC and XCI. (Pages 100, 101, 121 and 153.)

COLLANTES, FRANCISCO.—Spanish. Born in Madrid in 1599; died in 1656, probably in Madrid.—One picture in HALL XC. (Page 151.)

CORREA DE VIVAR, JUAN.—Spanish. A Castilian. He worked about the middle of the 16th. century.—Eight pictures in HALLS LXXIV and LXXV. (Page 123.)

CORREGGIO, IL (ANTONIO ALLEGRI).—Italian. Born in Correggio in 1493; died there in 1534.—Two pictures in HALL V. (Page 45.)

CRANACH *the Old*, LUCAS.—German. Born in Kronach in 1472; died at Weimar in 1553.—Two pictures in HALL XLIV. (Page 35.)

CRESPI, DANIELLE.—Italian. Born in Busto Arsizio about 1592; died in Milan in 1630.—One picture in HALL LXXXII and another in HALL LXXXIII. (Page 141.)

DAVID, GERARD.—Flemish. Born in Oudewater between 1450 and 1460; died in Bruges in 1523.—Three pictures in HALL XLII. (Page 31.)

DOMENICHINO, IL (DOMENICO ZAMPIERI).—Italian. Born in Bologna in 1581; died in Naples in 1641.—One picture in HALL LXXXV, and another in HALL LXXXVI. (Page 138.)

DÜRER, ALBRECHT.—German. Born in Nuremberg in 1471; died there in 1528.—Four pictures in HALL XLIV. (Pages 34 and 35.)

FLEMALLE, THE MASTER OF.—Flemish. Unknown painter of the first half of the 15th. century.—Four pictures in HALL XL. (Page 28.)

FORTUNY, MARIANO.—Spanish. Born in Reus in 1838; died in Rome in 1874.—Nine pictures in HALL LXXVI. (Page 132.)

FRANCES, MAESTRE NICOLÁS.—He worked in León before 1434; died in 1468.—One retable in HALL Ł. (Page 114.)

GADDI, TADEO.—Italian. Born in Florence in 1300; died there in 1367. Two panels in HALL IV. (Page 43.)

GALLEGO, FERNANDO.—Spanish.—He worked between 1466 and 1507.—One work in HALL XXIV. (Page 38.)

GARCIA DE BENABARRE, Pedro.—Spanish. Born probably in Benabarre (Huesca). He worked about the middle of the 15th. century.—Two panels in HALL L. (Page 114.)

GIORDANO, Lucca.—Italian. Born in 1632 in Naples, where he died in 1705.—Twenty seven pictures in HALLS LXXXI, LXXXVIII, LXXXIX and XCVI. (Page 140.)

GIORGIONE, Il (Giorgio da Castelfranco).—Italian. Born in Castelfranco Veneto about 1474; died in Venice in 1510.—One picture in HALL VI. (Page 46.)

GOSSAERT, Jan (or «Jan de Mabuse»).—Flemish. Born in Maubege about 1478; died between 1533 and 1536, probably in Middelbourg.—One picture in HALL XL, and two in HALL XLII. (Page 27.)

GOYA, Francisco.—Spanish. Born in Fuendetodos (Zaragoza) in 1746; died in Bordeaux in 1828.—Compositions and portraits in HALLS XXXII to XXXVI and XCV. «Cartoons» for tapestry in HALLS LV, LVI and LVII. Drawings in HALL XCVII. (Pages 103 to 109, 129 to 131, 155 and 156.)

GRECO, El (Domenikos Theotokopoulos).—A Greek who lived in Spain. Born in Crete in 1541; died in Toledo in 1614.—Thirty two pictures in HALL XXX. (Pages 60 to 65.)

GREUZE, Jean Baptiste.—French. Born in Tournus in 1725; died in Paris in 1805.—One picture in HALL XLIX. (Page 126.)

GUERCINO, Il (Francesco Giovanni Barbieri).—Italian. Born in Cento in 1591; died in Bologna in 1665.—Two pictures in HALL LXXXIII, and one in HALL LXXXVI. (Pages 141 and 142.)

HERRERA *the Old*, Francisco de.—Spanish. Born in Sevilla about 1576; died in Madrid in 1656.—Two pictures in HALL XCII. (Page 154.)

HERRERA *the Young*, Francisco de.—Spanish. Born in Sevilla in 1622; died in Madrid in 1685.—One picture in HALL XXIX. (Page 102.)

HOBBEMA, Meindert.—Dutch. Born in Amsterdam in 1638; died there in 1709.—One landscape in HALL LXIII. (Page 118.)

HOUASSE, Michel-Ange.—French. Born in Paris in 1680; died in Arpajon in 1730.—Four pictures in HALLS XLVIII, XLIX and LIII. (Page 127.)

HUGUET, Jaime.—Spanish. He painted in Barcelona between 1448 and 1487. One panel in HALL L. (Page 115.)

JORDAENS, Jacob.—Flemish. Born in 1593 in Antwerp where he died in 1678.—Eight pictures in HALL XVIII. (Pages 94 and 95.)

JUANES, Juan de (Vicente Juan Masip).—Spanish. Born probably in Fuente de la Higuera (Valencia) about 1523; died in Bocairente in 1579.—Eleven pictures in HALLS XXV, LXX and LXXV. (Pages 66 and 67.)

KAUFFMANN, Angelica.—German. Born in Chur (Switzerland) in 1741; died in Rome in 1807.—One portrait in HALL LXXX. (Page 136.)

LEONARDO, Jusepe.—Spanish. Born in Calatayud about 1605; died in Zaragoza in 1656.—Two pictures in HALL I and one in HALL XCI. (Page 153.)

LOPEZ, Vicente.—Spanish. Born in Valencia in 1772; died in Madrid in 1850.—One ceiling in HALL XXXIX, and thirteen portraits in HALLS XXXIX and XXXI. (Pages 111 and 112.)

LORRAINE, Claude de (Claude Gellée).—French. Born in a castle near Mirecourt in 1600; died in Rome in 1682.—Ten landscapes in HALLS XLVIII, LIII and LIV. (Page 126.)

LOTTO, Lorenzo.—Italian. Born in Venice in 1480; died in Loreto in 1556.—Two pictures in HALL VI. (Page 46.)

LUINI, Bernardino.—Italian. Born in Luino (Lombardy) between 1480 and 1485; died in 1532.—Two pictures in HALL V. (Page 45.)

MACHUCA, Pedro.—Spanish. Born in Toledo, towards the end of the 15th. century; died in Granada in 1550.—One picture in HALL XXV. (Page 66.)

MADRAZO, Federico de.—Spanish. Born in Rome in 1815; died in Madrid in 1894.—Three portraits in HALL LXXVII. (Pages 132 and 133.)

MADRAZO, Raimundo de.—Spanish. Born in Rome in 1841; died in Versailles in 1920.—Ten pictures in HALLS LXXVI and LXXVII. (Page 132.)

MAELLA, Mariano Salvador.—Spanish. Born in Valencia in 1739; died in Madrid in 1819.—Eight pictures in HALL XXXI. (Page 110.)

MAINO, Fray Juan Bautista.—Spanish. Born in the Milanesado in 1568; died in Madrid in 1649.—Three pictures in HALL XXV. (Page 69.)

MANTEGNA, Andrea.—Italian. Born in Isola di Cartura (Padova) in 1431; died in Mantua in 1506.—One picture in HALL IV. (Page 43.)

MARTINEZ DEL MAZO, Juan Bautista.—Spanish. Born probably in Beteta about 1620; died in Madrid in 1667.—Eight pictures in HALLS XI, XIII, XXIX and LXXXVIII. (Pages 103 and 144.)

MASIP, Vicente Juan.—Spanish. Born about 1475 in Valencia; died between 1545 and 1550.—Three pictures in HALL LXXV. (Page 123.)

MEISSONIER, Jean Louis Ernest.—French. Born in Lyons in 1815; died in Paris in 1891.—One portrait in HALL LXXVI. (Page 132.)

MELENDEZ, Luis Eugenio.—Spanish. Born in Naples in 1716; died in Madrid in 1780.—Twelve still-life pictures in HALL XXXI. (Page 110.)

MELENDEZ, Miguel Jacinto.—Spanish. Born in Oviedo in 1679; died about 1731.—Two pictures in HALL LXXXIX. (Page 146.)

ROMNEY, GEORGE.—English. Born in Dalton-le-Furness (Lancashire) in 1734; died in Kendal in 1802. — One portrait in HALL LXXXIV. (Page 143.)

RUBENS, PETER PAUL.—Flemish. Born in Siegen (Westfalia) in 1577; died in Antwerp in 1640.—Seventy-seven pictures in HALLS XVI, XVIII, XIX, XX, XXIII, XLVI and LXVII. (Pages 90 to 96 and 120.)

SANCHEZ COELLO, ALONSO.—Spanish. Born in Benifayó (Valencia) in 1531 or 1532; died in Madrid in 1588.—Ten pictures in HALLS XXV, LXXII and LXXV. (Pages 67 and 122.)

SARTO, ANDREA DEL.—Italian. Born in 1486, in Florence, where he died in 1531.—Eight pictures in HALLS V and LXXXVII. (Page 44.)

SASSOFERRATO, IL (GIOVANNI BATTISTA SALVI).—Italian. Born in Sassoferrato in 1605; died in Rome in 1685.—Two pictures in HALL LXXXVI. (Page 137.)

SEVILLA, JUAN DE.—Spanish. Born in 1643, in Granada, where he died in 1695.—One picture in HALL XCI. (Page 154.)

SIGÜENZA, MASTER OF.—Spanish. Unknown painter of the second quarter of the XVth. century.—Pieces from a retable in HALL L. (Page 114.)

SISLA, MASTER OF THE.—Spanish. Unknown painter who worked between the end of the XVth. and beginning of the next century.—Two pictures in HALL LXXV. (Page 123.)

SNAYERS, PEETER.—Flemish. Born in Antwerp in 1592; died in Brussels after the year 1667.—Sixteen pictures in HALLS LI, LXI, LXXII and LXXXVIII. (Page 117.)

SNYDERS, FRANS.—Flemish. Born in 1579, in Antwerp, where he died in 1657.—Seventeen pictures in HALLS LXII, LXIV, LXV, LXVI, LXVIII and LXIX. (Page 119.)

STANZIONE, IL CAVALIERE MASSIMO.—Italian. Born in Naples in 1585; died in 1656.—Five pictures in HALL LXXXIII. (Page 142.)

STROZZI, BERNARDO.—Italian. Born in Genoa in 1581; died in Venice in 1644.—One picture in HALL LXXXVI. (Page 138.)

SUSTERMAN, JUSTUS.—Flemish. Born in Antwerp in 1597; died in Florence in 1681.—Two portraits in HALL LXI. (Page 117.)

TENIERS, DAVID.—Flemish. Born in Antwerp in 1610; died in Brussels in 1690.—Twenty five pictures in HALLS LXV, XLVI and XCVI. (Page 119.)

TIEPOLO, GIOVANNI BATTISTA.—Italian. Born in Venice in 1696; died in Madrid in 1770.—Seven pictures in HALL XXXIX. (Page 111.)

TIEPOLO, GIOVANNI DOMENICO.—Italian. Born in 1727 in Venice, where he died in 1804.—Eight pictures in HALLS XXXI, LXXXI and LXXXIV. (Pages 110 and 143.)

TINTORETTO, IL (JACOPO ROBUSTI).—Italian. Born probably in 1518, in Venice, where he died in 1594.—Twenty four pictures in HALLS VI, X, LXXXV, LXXXVI, and LXXXVII. (Pages 57, 58, 59 and 138.)

TITIAN, VECELLIO DI GREGORIO.—Italian. Born in Cadore in 1477; died in Venice in 1576.—Seven pictures in HALL VI, seven in HALL VIII, sixteen in HALL IX, two in HALL XLV and one in HALL LXXXVI. (Pages 46, 47, 49 to 56 and 138.)

TRISTAN, LUIS.—Spanish. Born late in the XVIth century; died in Toledo in 1624.—Two pictures in HALL LXXXIX. (Page 145.)

VALDES LEAL, JUAN DE.—Spanish. Born in 1622 in Sevilla, where he died in 1690.—Four pictures in HALLS LXXIV, XC and XCI. (Pages 121 and 122.)

VAN DYCK, ANTON.—Flemish. Born in Antwerp in 1599; died in Black-fiars (London) in 1641.—Twenty-five pictures in HALLS XVI, XVII, XVIII, XIX, LXVII and LXXIX. (Pages 93, 94 and 120.)

VAN HEMESEN, JAN SANDERS.—Flemish. Born in Hemixen about 1500; died in Harlem, about 1565.—One picture in HALL XLIV. (Page 36.)

VAN LOO, LOUIS MICHEL.—French. Born in Toulon in 1707; died in Paris in 1771.—Four pictures in HALLS XLIX and LIII. (Page 127.)

VAN ORLEY, BAREND.—Flemish. Born about 1492 in Brussels, where he died in 1542.—Three pictures in HALLS XL, XLI and XLII. (Page 31.)

VAN OSTADE, ADRIAEN.—Dutch. Born in 1610 in Harlem, where he died in 1684.—Four pictures in HALL LXIII. (Page 118.)

VAN UTRECHT, ADRIAEN.—Flemish. Born in 1599 in Antwerp, where he died in 1652.—Three pictures in HALLS XX and LXVI. (Page 119.)

VAN DER WEYDEN, ROGER (OR ROGER DE LA PASTURE).—Flemish. Born in Tournai about 1399; died in Brussels in 1464.—Eight pictures in HALLS XL, XLI and XCII. (Pages 29 and 30.)

VELAZQUEZ, DIEGO RODRÍGUEZ DE SILVA.—Spanish. Born in Sevilla in 1599; died in Madrid in 1660.—Eight pictures in HALL XI, twenty-seven in HALL XII, nine in HALL XIII, one in HALL XV and one in HALL XXIX. (Pages 74 to 89.)

VERONESE, IL (PAOLO CALIARI).—Italian. Born in Verona, probably in 1528; died in Venice in 1588.—Eight pictures in HALL VII, and five in HALL VIII. (Pages 47 to 51.)

VOS, PAUL DE.—Flemish. Born in Huls in 1596; died in Antwerp in 1678.—Nine pictures of animals in HALLS LXI, LXV and LXVIII. (Page 117.)

WATTEAU, JEAN ANTOINE.—French. Born in Valenciennes in 1684; died in Nogent-sur-Marne in 1721.—Two pictures in HALL LIV. (Page 129.)

YAÑEZ DE LA ALMEDINA, Fernando.—Spanish. Born probably in La Almedina (Ciudad Real), and worked during the first half of the XVIth. century.—Two pictures in HALL XXV and one in HALL LXXV. (Page 66.)

ZURBARAN, Francisco de.—Spanish. Born in Fuente de Cantos (Badajoz) in 1598; died in Madrid in 1664.—Eight pictures in HALL XXVI. (Pages 71 to 73.)